2/03

FROM ATALANTA TO ZEUS

FROM ATALANTA TO ZEUS

Readers Theatre from Greek Mythology

Suzanne I. Barchers

2001
TEACHER IDEAS PRESS
A Division of
Libraries Unlimited, Inc.
Englewood, Colorado

Dedicated to Karyn Estela,
who outshines the Muses

TEACHER IDEAS PRESS
A Division of
Libraries Unlimited, Inc.
P.O. Box 6633
Englewood, CO 80155-6633
1-800-237-6124
www.lu.com/tip

Library of Congress Cataloging-in-Publication Data

Barchers, Suzanne I.
    From Atalanta to Zeus : readers theatre from Greek mythology / Suzanne I. Barchers.
        p. cm.
    Includes bibliographical references (p.) and index.
    ISBN 1-56308-815-0 (softbound)
    1. Mythology, Greek--Juvenile drama. 2. Children's plays, American. [1. Mythology, Greek--Drama. 2. Readers' theater. 3. Plays.] I. Title.

PS3552.A5988 F76 2001
812'.54--dc21
                                                            2001018121

 **CONTENTS**

INTRODUCTION

Greek gods and mythical heroes, from Atalanta to Zeus, have inspired story-tellers for centuries, and their stories provide an ideal venue for readers theatre. Although drawn from the Greek myths, many readers of this volume will recognize elements that occur in a variety of legends and stories. For example, "Eros and Psyche" has a strong parallel with "Cupid and Psyche" and may even remind students of "Beauty and the Beast." The introductions to many of the scripts here discuss additional parallels. Choosing the stories for this collection proved to be a challenging process. There seems to be an endless supply of stories or story fragments and a vast number of mortal and immortal characters. Some stories, such as those of the heroes Jason and Odysseus, are lengthy and could not be fully developed in one script. In other cases, minor characters, such as Pandora, may be familiar because the character plays a pivotal role in the stories. The character may only warrant a small role in a larger story, however. Therefore, if a favorite character is missing from the table of contents, check the index to determine if that hero's story is included in a larger story.

The lives of these gods are often complex and bewildering. Legends provide varying names for parentage, offspring, locales, and so forth. (See the bibliography for the sources consulted throughout the development of the scripts.) In many cases, decisions about details were based on the most frequent uses found in the resources or were simply arbitrary. Deciding how to treat the behaviors of the characters proved to be another challenge. Many of them, both mortal and immortal, were not always exemplary. Several abandoned their children. Zeus, although married to Hera, would often take on disguises to seduce women he favored. Therefore, he had many children, often with beautiful mortal women. Oedipus, famous for killing his father and marrying his mother, actually did not knowingly set out to behave inappropriately, and his story is included because of the misconceptions surrounding this compelling myth. The scripts treat practices such as multiple marriages or liaisons as delicately as possible, and it is assumed that the students will have some familiarity with the stories and practices in general. Teachers are advised to always preread a script to ensure that it is appropriate for the grade level and background knowledge of their students.

Using Readers Theatre

Readers theatre can be compared to radio plays. The emphasis is on an effective reading of the script rather than on a dramatic, memorized presentation. Students may paraphrase the scripts, and this should be encouraged. Because of the many challenging names and places, the pronunciation guide should be consulted when rehearsing the reading. In some scripts, the narrators have long passages, and they should rehearse their lines carefully. Reading orally develops strong reading skills, and listening to scripts promotes active listening for students in the audience.

The scripts also provide an opportunity for preparing a special program or for a diversion from the regular curriculum. Scripts can be used to introduce or close a unit on Greece or Greek mythology. Subject area teachers and librarians can collaborate using readers theatre for social studies literature.

Preparing the Scripts

Once you have chosen scripts for reading, make enough copies for each character, plus an extra set or two for your use and a replacement copy. To help readers keep their places, have students use highlighter markers to designate their character's role within the copy. For example, someone reading the role of Narrator 1 could highlight the lines in blue, with another character highlighting the lines in yellow.

Photocopied scripts will last longer if you use a three-hole punch (or copy them on prepunched paper) and place them in inexpensive folders. The folders can be color-coordinated to the internal highlighting for each character's part. The title of the play can be printed on the outside of the folder, and scripts can be stored easily for the next reading. The preparation of the scripts is a good project for a student aide or volunteer parent. The preparation takes a minimum of initial attention and needs to be repeated only when a folder is lost.

Getting Started

For the first experience with a readers theatre script, choose a script with many characters to involve more students. Gather the students informally. If possible, read aloud a narrative of the myth from one of the titles in the bibliography. Next, introduce the script and explain that readers theatre does not mean memorizing a play and acting it out, but rather reading a script aloud, perhaps with a few props and actions. Select volunteers to do the initial reading, allowing them an opportunity to review their parts before reading aloud. Discuss how the scripts are alike or different from the myth you've shared or that the students have heard. Write pronunciations on the board of any challenging words. While these students are preparing to read their script, another group could review another script or brainstorm ideas for props or staging.

Before reading the first script, decide whether to choose parts after the reading or to introduce additional scripts to involve more students. Consider holding a readers theatre workshop periodically, with each student belonging to a group that prepares a script for presentation. Students could also plan a readers theatre festival for a special day when several short scripts are presented consecutively, with brief intermissions between each reading. Consider grouping together related scripts. For example, "Aeolus and the Winds," a script about the behavior of the winds, could be paired with "Eos, Slene, and Helios," a script about the dawn, moon, and sun.

Once the students have read the scripts and become familiar with the new vocabulary, determine which students will read the various parts. Some parts are considerably more demanding than others, and students should be encouraged to volunteer for roles that will be comfortable for them. Once they are familiar with readers theatre, students should be encouraged to stretch and try a reading that is challenging. Reading scripts is especially useful for remedial reading students. Nonetheless, it is equally important that the students enjoy the literature.

Presentation Suggestions

For readers theatre, the participants traditionally stand—or sit on stools, chairs, or the floor—in a formal presentation style. The narrators usually stand with the script placed on music stands or lecterns slightly off to one or both sides. The readers hold their scripts in black or colored folders.

The position of the reader indicates the importance of the role. For example, Helen, Menelaus, and Paris are key characters and should be placed in the center, with the other characters flanking them. On occasion, key characters might sit on high stools to elevate them above numerous other characters. The scripts include a few suggestions for positioning readers, but students should be encouraged to create interesting arrangements. For long scripts, chairs or stools keep readers from tiring.

Props

Readers theatre has no, or few, props. Nonetheless, simple costuming effects, such as royal clothing or flowing gowns, plus a few props on stage will lend interest to the presentation. Suggestions for simple props or costuming are included; however, the students should be encouraged to decide how much or little to add to their reading. For some readers, the use of props or actions may be distracting, and the emphasis should remain on the reading rather than on an overly complicated presentation.

Delivery Suggestions

Delivery suggestions are not imbedded in the scripts but are provided in the introduction. Therefore, it is important to discuss with the students how they can make the scripts come alive as they read. During their first experiences with presenting a script, students are tempted to keep their heads buried in the script, making sure they don't miss a line. Students should learn the material well enough to look up from the script during the presentation. They can learn to use onstage focus, that is, to look at each other during the presentation. This is most logical for characters who are interacting with each other. The use of offstage focus, in which the presenters look directly into the eyes of the audience, is more logical for the narrator, who is uninvolved with onstage characters. Alternatively, have students who do not interact with each other focus on a prearranged offstage location, such as the classroom clock, during delivery. Simple actions can also be incorporated into readers theatre.

Generally, the audience should be able to see the readers' facial expressions during the reading. On occasion, it might seem logical for a character to move across the stage, facing the other characters while reading. In this event, the characters should be turned enough so that the audience can see their faces.

The Next Step

Once students have enjoyed the reading process involved in preparing and presenting readers theatre, the logical next step is to involve them in the writing process by creating their own scripts. Encourage students to research other myths or parallel myths. For example, the labors that Psyche faces are well documented in the Latin versions of her myth and would provide a logical extension of the script provided in this collection. Students also should be encouraged to research the clothing, lifestyles, art, and food of the ancient Greeks. This process will enhance both language arts and social studies. The bibliography provides resources for students and teachers to explore.

AEOLUS AND THE WINDS

After the great flood, Zeus asked Aeolus to take control of the winds that had wreaked havoc. Zeus feared that the winds would continue their destructive habits if left unchecked. Each of the winds has its own characteristics; in this short script, each wind describes its history. Consider pairing it with another script, "The Sisters, Dawn, Sun, and Moon." Students may want to research the role Aeolus played in other myths in which the deities directed him to either free or contain the winds.

Presentation Suggestions

Have the readers stand in the following order: Narrator, Aeolus, Boreas, Zephyrus, Notus, and Eureus. Each reader should step forward for the reading and step back when finished. Alternatively, have the readers remain seated when not reading their parts.

Props

Consider having the winds dress appropriately for their roles. Boreas could be in dark, heavy robes and have a windblown look. Zephyrus could be adorned with bright colors and flowers. Notus could be dressed in gray, perhaps carrying a large, dark umbrella. Eureus could be dressed in light colors.

Delivery Suggestions

Aeolus should have a normal reading voice. Boreas should have a loud, bombastic voice. Zephyrus should sound strong, though not as blustery as Boreas. Notus should sound dreary, and Eureus should sound pleasant and quiet.

Characters

- ▣ Narrator
- ▣ Aeolus
- ▣ Boreas
- ▣ Zephyrus
- ▣ Notus
- ▣ Eurus

AEOLUS AND THE WINDS

Narrator: During the great nine-day flood, the winds howled and raged cease-lessly. When their destructive forces threatened Olympus, Zeus realized that the winds needed a guardian. He solved this dilemma by appointing Aeolus as keeper of the winds. Listen as Aeolus and the winds tell you their stories.

Aeolus: When Zeus made me guardian of the winds, I knew they would need to be carefully controlled. Zeus sent us to live in a cave in a cliff, far out at sea. The winds, if left to their own will, would rage at the slightest whim, just to amuse themselves. But with me in control, they could only leave the cave when I would pierce the wall of the cliff with my spear. I'd let one wind out, closing up the hole until it returned so that no others could escape. Like any family, each wind had its individual characteristics.

Boreas: I am Boreas, although you may have heard of me as the North Wind. No one is stronger than I. With one blast, I can bring ice to the Earth, tear up trees, and cause floods. With just a bit of effort, I can even cause a tidal wave. I've had a variety of adventures and have many children. As you can imagine, all my offspring are fleet of foot. Once, at Iris's request, I fanned a funeral pyre. Sometimes I answer prayers, bringing weather that helps in battle. The Athenians were so grateful to me for helping them defeat the invader Xerxes that they built a temple in my honor. I enjoy being the most powerful—and sometimes the most dreaded—wind. The only wind who compares to me is my brother, Zephyrus, the West Wind.

Zephyrus: Yes, it is true that in ancient times I blustered when I blew. Many remember me for the discus incident with Hyacinthus. Here's the story, in case you haven't heard it. Many ages ago, Apollo and Hyacinthus were prac-ticing throwing the discus. Some people claim Boreas caused the discus to change direction, killing Hyacinthus. Others blame me, believing that I was jealous of Hyacinthus. The truth is that I *did* cause the discus to veer off course, but I never knew it would rebound off the rock and fatally wound Hyacinthus. I've mellowed since then, and when a storm is passing, you'll see me sweeping the sky clean so the sun can smile on everyone. If you travel along the road to Eleusis, you might see a temple in my name. But now you must hear about Notus, the South Wind.

Notus: You may have heard of my parents, Eos, the Dawn, and Astraeus. It's hard for me to be confined, for I am usually heavy with fog, dew, or rain. When Aeolus pierces the cliff wall, I have to squeeze my way out, and it's always a great relief to be able to spread out. Sometimes people curse me for bring-ing fog. Many a sailor has lost his way on the sea in an unexpected fog I have blown across the sea. Even travelers on foot have lost their way in my fogs. But I bring moisture to Earth, and often the mortals are particularly grateful for my life-giving rains. Without me, mortals would not appreciate the clear days after a storm nearly as much. And now, meet our last brother, Eurus, the East Wind.

Eurus: You won't find a temple named after me because I am rarely let out, and I have a modest effect. I'm not a destructive wind, and I don't bring rain or fog. If I got out more or could combine my strength with one of my brothers, mortals would remember me. Usually I come out on days that are pleasant enough, but not necessarily memorable. All in all, I'm just a pleasant wind you might encounter on any day.

Narrator: You'll hear about the winds in many of the stories, perhaps not by name, but rest assured that they are about. When a storm blows branches off your trees, you'll know that Boreas, the North Wind, has visited. When the skies are blown clean after the storm, you can thank Zephyrus, the West Wind. When the thirsty crops are watered by a welcome summer storm, you can praise Notus, the South Wind. And when you're just enjoying a gentle breeze on a spring day, give your appreciation to Eurus, the East Wind.

Ariadne, known as the High Fruitful Mother or Most Holy, showed great resourcefulness and courage. When fourteen Athenians arrived at Crete for the sacrifices to the Minotaur, Ariadne begged Daedalus to help her save Theseus. She had fallen in love with him and admired his courage. Ariadne took the magic ball of thread, giving it to Theseus in exchange for his promise to marry her and take her to Athens. But after their escape, Dionysus appeared to Theseus in a dream, telling him to leave Ariadne on the island of Naxos. Theseus abandoned Ariadne, who quickly succumbed to Dionysus's affections. They returned together to Olympus, and she eventually had four children with Dionysus.

Presentation Suggestions

The narrators should sit on either side of the stage. King Minos can sit in an ornate chair or on a high stool to one side. Theseus should have the king on one side and Ariadne on the other side. Dionysus should be on the other side of Ariadne. The minor characters, Daedalus and the Athenian, can be standing slightly behind the other characters.

Props

King Minos can wear a crown. Ariadne should be dressed as a princess. Theseus could carry a sword. The other characters can be dressed simply. Consider having a ball of yarn on the stage. Consider creating a backdrop that shows islands and sailing ships on the horizon.

Delivery Suggestions

Ariadne should sound persuasive when talking with King Minos and Daedalus. She should then sound angry when abandoned by Theseus. King Minos should sound autocratic and cold about the sacrifices. Theseus should sound confident and bold. Dionysus should sound reassuring and kind.

Characters

- ⊡ Narrator 1
- ⊡ Narrator 2
- ⊡ King Minos
- ⊡ Theseus
- ⊡ Ariadne
- ⊡ Daedalus
- ⊡ Athenian
- ⊡ Dionysus

ARIADNE

Narrator 1: Many years ago, King Minos enraged Poseidon, who had demanded that a white bull be sacrificed to him. But the king's wife, Pasiphaë, was entranced with the white bull and entreated King Minos to spare it. When King Minos honored his wife's wishes to let the white bull live, Poseidon punished them by causing Pasiphaë to give birth to a monster, the Minotaur. This monster ate nothing but human flesh.

Narrator 2: Daedalus constructed a labyrinth under the palace in Crete with a maze of passageways impossible to navigate. It kept the Minotaur imprisoned, and as long as it had enough flesh to eat, the monster was quiet.

Narrator 1: To keep the monster fed, King Minos had to raid nearby islands, bringing back fresh victims. But one day the tables were turned, and King Minos's son was accidentally killed while visiting Athens. King Minos seized upon this opportunity to threaten Athens with an attack unless they provided seven young women and seven young men as sacrifices for the Minotaur every nine years.

Narrator 2: The King of Athens, King Aegeus, consented, infuriating the Athenians who resented seeing their youth murdered. Twice, the sacrifice was paid. But as the third time approached, a young hero became known for his daring exploits. King Aegeus discovered the young man was in truth his son, Theseus, who volunteered to take the place of one of the next victims. He was confident that he could slay the Minotaur and stop the senseless sacrifices. His father agreed to let him try, and the seven young women and seven young men set sail for Crete.

Narrator 1: King Minos and Pasiphaë had a lovely daughter, Ariadne, and with the arrival of the fourteen victims, our story of Ariadne truly begins.

King Minos: Bring the victims to me! I want to ensure that they are indeed going to satisfy the Minotaur. Who speaks for the group?

Theseus: I speak for the Athenians. We are prepared to meet the Minotaur, but I request that you let us go with honor.

King Minos: What do you mean by that request?

Theseus: I only ask that you let me take my sword with me.

King Minos: That will hardly save you from the Minotaur, but go ahead if you think it will bring you honor.

Narrator 2: Ariadne was quite taken with Theseus's confidence and demeanor. She despised the thought that he was destined to die to satisfy this gruesome beast's appetites.

Ariadne: Father, why must we sacrifice these fine young people?

King Minos: You know why, my daughter. If the Minotaur doesn't eat regularly, he will plague us with his howling. Try not to think about it.

Narrator 1: But Ariadne couldn't stop thinking about the handsome young Athenian. She realized that she had fallen in love with him. That night, she went to see Daedalus to request his assistance.

Ariadne: Daedalus, I need your help.

Daedalus: Of course, I will do anything in my power to help you.

Ariadne: I don't want to see Theseus and the other Athenians killed by the Minotaur. Theseus has a sword, but even if he manages to kill the Minotaur, how would he find his way out of the labyrinth?

Daedalus: That is easy to remedy. Take this magic ball of thread. Tell Theseus to tie the end to the gate and to let it out as he enters the labyrinth. Then he can find his way out.

Ariadne: Thank you, Daedalus. I'll be forever in your debt if this works.

Narrator 2: Later, Ariadne sneaked to the prison so that she could speak to Theseus.

Ariadne: Theseus, I have come to help you escape the labyrinth. You'll have to kill the Minotaur on your own, but if you succeed, I can get you out.

Theseus: How can you do that?

Ariadne: There is a way, but before I tell you, you must make me a promise.

Theseus: What is that?

Ariadne: I want you to marry me and take me back to Athens with you.

Theseus: If I escape, I will gladly marry you. Our ship is waiting for us to escape, and then you can return with me.

Ariadne: Then here is what you do. Take this magic ball of thread. Tie the end to the gate when you enter. Keep unrolling it as you search for the Minotaur. When you are ready to escape, you can follow it back.

Theseus: Thank you Ariadne. This will be a great help. You are as clever as you are beautiful.

Narrator 1: Theseus carefully tied the ball of thread to the gate. As soon as he set the ball down, it began to unroll, leading him through the winding passageways and up and down the stairs. Theseus followed it until he heard the snoring of the Minotaur. He wasted no time in attacking the monster. The monster roared so loudly that the island shook. But Theseus had surprised the monster. He leaped at the Minotaur, killing it with his bare hands. He followed the thread back to the gate where Ariadne waited for him.

Ariadne: You made it! Let's free the others and then set sail for Athens.

Theseus: Thank you, Ariadne, but first we have to ensure that your father doesn't follow us.

Ariadne: I have an idea. Have some of the men go to my father's ships and bore holes in them. That will slow them down, and we will be able to escape.

Narrator 2: They soon set sail. Theseus was delighted at bringing back a beautiful bride, but in the middle of the first night of the return journey, he had a disturbing dream. He went to one of his fellow Athenians to discuss it.

Theseus: I have had the most distressing dream.

Athenian: Tell me about it, Theseus.

Theseus: I dreamed that Dionysus spoke to me. It was so real that it seemed like he was here on the ship.

Athenian: What did he say?

Theseus: He told me that I was forbidden to marry Ariadne, and he insisted that I set her ashore on the island of Naxos.

Athenian: You have no choice, Theseus. If Dionysus truly wants Ariadne, he'll let nothing stand in his way of getting her.

Theseus: But I promised to marry her, and I've grown to love her.

Athenian: Do you want to jeopardize all our lives? You have no choice.

Narrator 1: When they arrived at Naxos, Theseus suggested that everyone go ashore and rest. Ariadne fell into a deep sleep, and while she slept, Theseus and the others slipped away. Soon Ariadne woke up and saw a young god approaching her.

Ariadne: Where is everyone? And who are you?

Dionysus: I am Dionysus, and you have been sleeping soundly. How did you get here?

Ariadne: My father is King Minos, and I helped Theseus and the other Athenians escape from the Minotaur in the labyrinth. Theseus promised to marry me, but now I am here alone.

Dionysus: Theseus is not worthy of you. Look, his ship is nearing the horizon as he returns without you. Come with me, and I'll take you to Olympus where you'll rule alongside me.

Narrator 2: Ariadne was enchanted with the handsome god and agreed to return with him. When they married, Dionysus presented her with a golden diadem made by Hephaestus. This gift later became a constellation.

Narrator 1: Ariadne had four children, named Thoas, Staphylus, Oenopion, and Peparethus. She lived a long life alongside her husband.

ARTEMIS AND NIOBE

Artemis is also known as Diana in Latin. Niobe, known as "Snowy One," was an Anatolian Mountain goddess married to Amphion, king of Thebes. In this script, Artemis asks Zeus to allow her to remain unmarried so that she can devote herself to hunting. She also enjoys bathing with her entourage of nymphs. When she does show some romantic interest in another god, her brother Apollo ensures that the god is killed. Artemis and Apollo are fiercely defensive of their mother, Leto, and when Niobe boasts that she has more children than Leto has, Apollo and Artemis kill her seven sons and seven daughters. (Note that in some sources, Leto is reported to have six sons and six daughters.)

Presentation Suggestion

Artemis and Niobe should stand in the center, toward the front of the stage. Zeus and Narrator 1 should stand to the side of Artemis, with Apollo and Narrator 2 on the other side. The narrators could be seated on chairs or stools, with the other characters standing.

Props

Students can capitalize on the woodland setting for this script, using plants or a mural of a forest scene to decorate the stage. If available, a small fountain could be added, giving the listeners a background of water sounds. A tape or compact disc of water sounds could be used alternatively. The stage could also have bows and quivers of arrows on it.

Delivery Suggestions

Artemis should vary her delivery to correspond with her exchanges with the various characters. For example, when talking with Zeus, she should sound respectful, but when dealing with Niobe, she should sound disdainful and powerful. Actaeon should speak quietly when he spies on Artemis and the nymphs. Apollo has a rather devious role when he tricks Artemis into killing Orion and should also vary his presentation appropriately. Niobe should sound haughty at first, then despairing over the deaths of her sons, and finally resume her haughtiness.

Characters

- ◙ Narrator 1
- ◙ Artemis
- ◙ Zeus
- ◙ Leto
- ◙ Narrator 2
- ◙ Actaeon
- ◙ Apollo
- ◙ Niobe

ARTEMIS AND NIOBE

Narrator 1: As a young goddess, Artemis knew exactly what kind of life she wanted to lead. She had no use for marriage but wanted to stay young, hunt with friends, and enjoy the outdoors. She went to her father, Zeus, and her mother, Leto, with a request that they found difficult to refuse.

Artemis: Father, I have a wish I hope you will grant.

Zeus: What would that be, Artemis?

Artemis: You know how I enjoy the woods and hunting. I have no interest in becoming an adult and marrying. Would you promise that I can stay young forever, hunt through the woods, and never be forced to marry?

Zeus: Are you sure this is what you want, my daughter?

Artemis: Yes, father.

Zeus: What do you think about this, Leto?

Leto: Well, I know how happy you are when hunting.

Artemis: I have tried to enjoy other pursuits, but they aren't for me.

Leto: What if you change your mind later?

Artemis: I don't think I will, Mother.

Leto: Then I have no objections to her request, Zeus.

Zeus: My daughter, I shall grant your wish and hope that it makes you happy.

Artemis: Thank you Father and Mother, but I have one other request, which you should find easy to grant.

Zeus: And what is that?

Artemis: I would like to have fifty nymphs as companions and a pack of hounds for hunting.

Zeus: Why not, Artemis? You seem determined to have your way, and at least you'll have some company.

Narrator 2: Artemis took great pleasure hunting with the nymphs and her hounds. They would hunt for hours, and Artemis became increasingly skilled with her bow and arrows. After a hunt, Artemis and her companions would refresh themselves by bathing in any available pool.

Narrator 1: One night Actaeon, a young mortal hunter, happened upon a pool near the Parthenius fountain where Artemis and her nymphs were bathing. Accompanied by his hounds, he quietly approached and watched.

Actaeon: What have we here? What a bounty of lovely bathers. I must get a better look at them.

Narrator 2: Actaeon slipped closer to the pool, keeping as quiet as possible.

Actaeon: Ah, there's a young woman who must be the most beautiful of all, one worthy of my attention and devotion. She must be a goddess, but I am compelled to speak with her.

Narrator 1: Mesmerized by Artemis's beauty, Actaeon continued to gaze at her until she realized his presence. Immediately she covered herself while reaching for the silvery water. She threw the water at Actaeon, and as the drops hit his forehead, he sprouted antlers on his head. In moments Actaeon was transformed into a stag.

Artemis: Now you will learn not to spy on bathers!

Narrator 2: With those words, Actaeon's dogs turned on the stag, never realizing it was their master. Soon Actaeon was dead.

Artemis: No mortal shall see me bathing and live! Let that be a lesson to others who might try!

Narrator 1: For a time, Artemis seemed content with her hunting and companions. Then she became acquainted with Orion, and she began to think that perhaps marriage could be acceptable, perhaps even pleasant.

Narrator 2: But her brother, Apollo, was jealous of any romantic attachments Artemis might consider. He contrived to ensure that Artemis and Orion would not ever marry.

Apollo: Artemis, do you see something far out in the sea?

Artemis: Of course I do. Why?

Apollo: I hear that you are especially accurate with a bow and arrow. Perhaps you would like to prove it.

Artemis: A-ha, a challenge! Is that perhaps my target?

Apollo: Only if you think you can hit something so very far away.

Artemis: That shouldn't trouble me at all, brother.

Narrator 1: Without hesitation, Artemis removed an arrow from her quiver and shot it from her bow far across the sea. The arrow found its mark, piercing Orion's temple, killing him. Now Artemis would never lose her heart to him.

Narrator 2: Artemis was angry at first, but she soon forgave her brother. Artemis and Apollo became increasingly close, both adoring their mother, Leto, and remaining very protective of her. One day they overheard Niobe, queen of Thebes, boasting to her people.

Niobe: Why worship Leto? My father is Tantalus, the only mortal who has eaten at the same table with Zeus! My mother, Dione, is sister to the Pleiades, the most brilliant constellation in the heavens. My ancestor Atlas carried the weight of the heavens on his shoulders. And I am married to Amphion, King of Thebes! Let us not forget that I have seven sons and seven daughters, and Leto has only one son and one daughter. Just think, I'll soon have seven sons- and seven daughters-in-law! My people, forget Leto. I implore you to build me a temple worthy of my fine family.

Artemis: Apollo, have you heard of Niobe's vain desires? She thinks that she deserves a temple just because she has fourteen children! That wretched Niobe should not be allowed to slander Leto.

Apollo: We can fix that for her! Let's use our arrows and bring an end to her family.

Narrator 1: Apollo used his arrows on the sons, killing them all. Niobe was overwhelmed with this tragic assault and threw herself on the ground, lamenting to the gods who were watching.

Niobe: Look at me, Leto, and you will see that I am miserable. You've driven me to despair. How will I survive this devastation?

Narrator 2: At that moment, Niobe saw her seven daughters approaching in their mourning garments. She forgot her peril and resumed her haughty attitude.

Niobe: At least I have my seven daughters. Few can boast of such a richness.

Narrator 1: Of course, Artemis heard Niobe's foolish words and loosed a quiver of arrows on the innocent young maidens. Each fell from the painless arrows, while Niobe watched in disbelief.

Narrator 2: Niobe sat alone, surrounded by the bodies of her beloved children. Her heart turned cold with grief, and the blood stopped pulsing through her veins. Soon she was still, turning to stone except for the tears that wash down her marble cheeks to this day.

ATALANTA

Abandoned at birth by her parents, Iasus and Clymene, Atalanta was raised by bears and later rescued by a hunter who taught her the ways of mortals. When Atalanta found fame as a runner and marksman, her parents reclaimed her. Her father decided she must have a husband, and Atalanta insisted that she would only marry a man who could beat her in a race. All those she defeated would lose their lives. Melanion, son of Onchestus, received help from Aphrodite and distracted Atalanta during the race by tossing down golden apples. He won the race, and they married. They neglected to pay proper homage to Aphrodite, however, and shortly thereafter, Aphrodite turned the couple into lions.

Presentation Suggestions

The characters should stand in the following order: Narrator 1, Iasus, Clymene, Meleager, Atalanta, Melanion, and Narrator 2. Iasus and Clymene may sit on chairs.

Props

Iasus and Clymene could be dressed in royal clothing. Atalanta can be dressed simply, perhaps in a short tunic appropriate for running and hunting. She could have a bow and several arrows at her feet. Melanion could also be dressed in clothing that would allow running.

Delivery Suggestions

Iasus should sound authoritative and controlling. Clymene should sound distressed at the prospect of losing her daughter. Atalanta should sound young and independent. Melanion should sound confident.

Characters

- ◙ Narrator 1
- ◙ Iasus
- ◙ Clymene
- ◙ Narrator 2
- ◙ Meleager
- ◙ Atalanta
- ◙ Melanion

ATALANTA

Narrator 1: Iasus and Clymene were two mortals who desperately wanted a son. When their first child proved to be a girl, Iasus called Clymene to him.

Iasus: Clymene, I was disappointed to receive the news that our child was not the son I had wanted.

Clymene: But she's a beautiful child, Iasus.

Iasus: That may be, but the fact remains that a daughter is useless to me.

Clymene: I disagree, my husband, but surely the gods will bless us with a son in time.

Iasus: Perhaps, but for now she will only cause trouble. If the gods see that we have this child, they may not bless us with a son. There is only one thing to do. I am going to have her taken to the forest to die. She's little and won't last long when left outside.

Clymene: Please, can't you reconsider?

Iasus: No, my mind is made up.

Narrator 2: The child was abandoned on a mountaintop. A bear found the baby and then used her gentle paws to carry her to her den. There the bear nursed her and raised her with her cubs. The child was comfortable in the woods and grew to be fleet of foot.

Narrator 1: One day a hunter saw her racing with the bears through the woods. The hunter set a snare, caught her, and took her home to finish her rearing. The hunter named her Atalanta. She was as clever as she was fast, and she soon mastered the language of mortals.

Narrator 2: Her foster father decided to put her in the athletic games that were popular at the time. Atalanta won many races and became famous for her conquests. Meanwhile, while she was winning races, Meleager, son of Oneneus, King of Calydon, faced a difficult challenge.

Narrator 1: Meleager had sailed on the Argo with Jason, and Meleager's skill with the spear was known throughout the world. His father, King Oeneus, had angered Artemis by forgetting to offer a sacrifice to her, and Artemis had retaliated by sending a huge boar to terrorize the countryside. King Oeneus asked Meleager to help him vanquish the boar. Meleager summoned a variety of heroes to help but was unprepared for Atalanta's arrival.

Meleager: Atalanta, what are you doing here? This hunt isn't for a girl.

Atalanta: I know how to handle a spear, and there's no one who can outrun me.

Meleager: That may be, but what will the others think of your participating in the hunt?

Atalanta: Do you want to be rid of the boar? It seems that you should be ready to accept all help, no matter the source.

Meleager: You have a good point. You can join us, but I can't spend time protecting you. You'll have to hold your own.

Atalanta: I don't expect to be treated any differently than the other hunters.

Narrator 2: Many heroes gathered for the hunt. After feasting and making the customary sacrifices, they drove the boar out of its lair. The boar roared forth, and before any spears and arrows could find a mark, seven men were dead. Atalanta ran after the boar, dodging through the trees until the boar tired and she could take careful aim. Suddenly, Meleager stepped in the path of the boar, preparing to throw his spear. His aim wasn't true, but Atalanta was in place. She stopped the boar with one arrow. Meleager realized that without her intervention, he surely would have been injured.

Meleager: Atalanta, the hide and tusks of this beast belong to you in appreciation for stopping the boar.

Atalanta: I am happy to be of service to you, Meleager.

Narrator 1: But not everyone was happy with the outcome. Meleager's two uncles taunted Meleager for letting the young woman save him. In his fury, Meleager killed them, enraging his mother. Unfortunately, she had a weapon of her own. At Meleager's birth, the Fates had told his mother that he would live only until a particular log burned up. For years his mother had hidden the log so that it couldn't be burned. In her anger, she removed the log from its hiding place and threw it into the fire. It burst into flames, and both the log and Meleager turned to ashes.

Narrator 2: Unknowingly, Atalanta happily continued on her way, taking along the trophies that proved she could outrun and outshoot the finest heroes of Greece. Before long, the story of her athletic prowess, as well as how she was found in the woods, reached Iasus and Clymene.

Iasus: Clymene, have you heard about this young woman who is rumored to be the fastest woman in any race?

Clymene: Yes, but what does that have to do with us?

Iasus: Clymene, I think she's the daughter we abandoned years ago. She's the right age, and it is said that bears raised her in the woods until a hunter rescued her.

Clymene: You mean our daughter is alive?

Iasus: Yes, and her name is Atalanta. I think it's time we meet this young lady and see if she could be our daughter. She is quite famous—you've heard how she killed the boar that was terrorizing Meleager's father. And if she is indeed ours, we will be made more famous for having brought her into this world.

Clymene: But how will you explain what we did?

Iasus: Don't worry about that. I'm sure she'll be so grateful to be part of our family that she won't question her past any more.

Narrator 1: Iasus summoned Atalanta to his palace. Her resemblance to Clymene was undeniable.

Iasus: Atalanta, tell us about your early years.

Atalanta: I grew up with a family of bears, but I don't know how I came to be with them. When I was nearly grown, a hunter caught me and took me into his home. He taught me how to live among mortals.

Iasus: Actually, you are of royal descent, Atalanta. You are our child, lost to us many years ago.

Atalanta: How can that be? What happened?

Iasus: Never mind, Atalanta. The important thing is that you are here now.

Narrator 2: Atalanta decided to stay with her parents. She began to enjoy her new family. Then one day Iasus summoned Atalanta to his throne.

Iasus: Atalanta, it's time you found yourself a husband.

Atalanta: I don't want to get married, Father.

Iasus: That may be, but it's tradition to get married, and you have to realize you're part of our royal family now.

Atalanta: Well, if I must marry, can we turn it into a contest?

Iasus: That sounds entertaining! What do you propose?

Atalanta: Why don't you let everyone know that I'll marry the man who can beat me in a running race.

Iasus: Atalanta, every young man in the world will want to race against you!

Atalanta: I don't think so, Father, when they hear that all who lose will lose their lives.

Iasus: You really *don't* want to marry, do you Atalanta?

Atalanta: No, Father, but if I must marry, at least this will keep the suitors to a manageable number.

Narrator 2: Not surprisingly, there were many young men so entranced with Atalanta that they were willing to risk their lives. As Atalanta had expected, they all lost their lives along with the races. Then one day Melanion arrived, well prepared to take up the challenge. He entered Atalanta's home and introduced himself.

Melanion: Atalanta, my name is Melanion, your future husband. Are you ready to race?

Atalanta: You're very sure of yourself, Melanion.

Melanion: I have good reason to be sure of myself, Atalanta. I'm going to win this race and win you as my bride.

Atalanta: I doubt it, but just to be sporting, I'll give you a head start.

Narrator 1: The race began, with Melanion in the lead. When Atalanta started running, she easily caught up with Melanion. But he quickly threw down a golden apple, given to him by Aphrodite, who had answered his prayers for help in winning the fair Atalanta.

Narrator 2: The golden apple looked so beautiful that Atalanta stopped to pick it up. Melanion kept running. When Atalanta overtook him, he threw a second apple off the racetrack. Atalanta left the track to retrieve the apple while

Melanion continued to run. When she once again closed the gap between them, Melanion threw the third golden apple far into the bushes.

Narrator 1: Atalanta had to have the third apple, and she dashed into the bushes to find it. Melanion raced across the finish line, winning the race as he'd predicted he would. Perhaps Atalanta truly wanted Melanion to claim her. As they looked upon each other at the race's end, Melanion happily claimed his prize.

Melanion: And now, Atalanta, will you be my wife?

Atalanta: Melanion, you have won the race, just as you said you would. I will keep my promise.

Narrator 2: The young couple lived happily together for many years. But they neglected to honor Aphrodite for bringing them together, and Aphrodite decided to punish them. Atalanta continued to run with her husband at her side, but Aphrodite had turned them into lions, destined to hunt in the woods for the rest of their lives.

ATHENA

Athena's name comes from the Sumerian *Anatha*, meaning queen of heaven. She is also known as Pallas, which means maiden in Greek. In this myth, Zeus fears that his first wife, Metis, will give birth to a son who will take away his throne. He tricks Metis into becoming a fly and swallows her whole. When Metis gives birth, her daughter Athena springs to life, fully grown, from Zeus's head. Athena becomes a just, although stern, ruler. She deals with the young mortal girl Arachne's boastful ways by turning her into a spider, and she successfully challenges Poseidon to gain control of Athens.

Presentation Suggestions

The two narrators can stand to one side, with Zeus next to them. Metis and Hephaestus can be next to Zeus, exiting or sitting down after their lines. Athena should be in the center of the stage, with Zeus on one side and Arachne and Poseidon on the other.

Props

Zeus, Metis, Hephaestus, Athena, and Poseidon can be dressed in robes or regal clothing. Athena could wear headgear to symbolize the helmet she is wearing when born. She could add a shawl over her head to disguise herself as the old woman. Hephaestus could carry a hammer. Arachne should be dressed in simple clothes, befitting a mortal. The stage could be decorated with a loom or with fake spider webs and plastic spiders commonly available at Halloween.

Delivery Suggestions

Zeus should sound powerful, but frustrated when the pounding begins in his head. Athena should change her voice, depending on her lines. When disguised as the old woman, she should sound appropriately old. When she reveals herself to Arachne, she should sound challenging and later angry. When dealing with Poseidon, she should sound confident.

Characters

- 回 Narrator 1
- 回 Narrator 2
- 回 Zeus
- 回 Metis
- 回 Hephaestus
- 回 Arachne
- 回 Athena
- 回 Poseidon

ATHENA

Narrator 1: Zeus ruled Mother Earth with great strength and power, but he longed to have another child. Although he had several wives, he appreciated the counsel and wisdom of his first wife, Metis, the goddess of prudence.

Narrator 2: But Mother Earth warned Zeus that if Metis gave birth to a son, the son would dethrone him in the same fashion that Zeus had dethroned his father, Cronus.

Zeus: I can't risk losing everything to a son, but I don't want to lose Metis altogether. I'll just have to trick her into staying with me in another form.

Narrator 1: Zeus called Metis to him and suggested that they play a game of changing shapes.

Zeus: Metis, I need some diversion. Let's play our shape-changing game.

Metis: What fun, Zeus! I'll begin the game by becoming a large animal!

Narrator 2: Metis changed into a lion, followed by a fox, and an assortment of animals of varying shapes and sizes.

Zeus: Well done, Metis, but can you become something very small?

Metis: Of course I can! Watch this!

Narrator 1: Metis changed herself into a fly, and in a heartbeat, Zeus opened wide his mouth and swallowed her whole!

Narrator 2: Metis realized she was trapped inside Zeus, so she decided to make the best of it. She settled herself in his head and whispered advice to him from within. But what he didn't realize was that Metis was soon to give birth to a daughter. While inside Zeus's head, she wove a robe and hammered out a helmet for the child.

Narrator 1: As you can imagine, the hammering gave Zeus a pounding headache. He called for the other gods to help him out of his misery. One who came was his son, Hephaestus, who was the god of smiths and fire.

Zeus: What am I to do about this intolerable pounding in my head?

Hephaestus: I can help you, but you'll have to trust me.

Zeus: Anything, Hephaestus, just stop this pounding.

Hephaestus: Give me a moment to use my tools, and the pain will soon be nothing but a memory.

Narrator 2: Hephaestus grasped his tools and split open his father's skull. Athena sprang out, wearing the robe and helmet Metis had created. Zeus was relieved to see that Metis had not borne him a son after all.

Narrator 1: Athena, known as the goddess of wisdom, devoted herself to just causes. She often led armies into battle, alongside Nike, the spirit of victory. During peaceful times she taught crafts and fine arts to others. Arachne, a simple mortal girl from the country who showed great talent with weaving, became one of Athena's favorite students. But Arachne was not always wise, and she took to boasting about her skills.

Arachne: My weaving is so beautiful that nothing compares with it. Not even Athena can exceed my talent!

Narrator 2: When Athena got word of Arachne's boastful ways, she disguised herself as an old woman and spoke to Arachne to see if the rumors were true.

Athena: Your work is lovely, young woman. You show great talent at weaving.

Arachne: Yes, my work gives me great pleasure, especially since it is finer than any other's work, even that of Athena's.

Athena: Why compare yourself to the gods when you can be the very best among mortals?

Arachne: Because I know I'm the best. If Athena thinks she is better, she can just come here and prove it!

Narrator 1: With that challenge in the air, Athena felt compelled to throw off her disguise and confront the foolish Arachne.

Athena: You are not only foolish, but you are also reckless. Let's settle this now with a competition. Sit down at your loom, and let's see just who is the best!

Narrator 2: The goddess and the mortal began to weave. Athena created a majestic portrayal of the gods of Olympus, while Arachne wove an impudent scene of Zeus and his wives. Athena was so appalled at Arachne's arrogance that she tore the tapestry to shreds and struck Arachne with her shuttle. Suddenly,

Arachne felt her head shrink to the size of a pea and her fingers change into long, nimble legs. She had been turned into a spider.

Athena: Impertinent girl, as a spider you can spin and weave forever and challenge no gods or mortals! I'll spare your life, though I could crush you in a moment. Get to work, little one! Weave forever.

Narrator 1: While Arachne worked, Athena, a stern goddess, watched from above. She knew that mortals must worship the gods, and she believed that Arachne's fate was just. She also enjoyed her role as a goddess and especially wanted to rule Athens, her favorite city in Greece.

Narrator 2: Unfortunately, Poseidon, lord of the sea, also wanted to control Athens. One day, as the two gods stood on the outskirts of the city, they decided they would settle the matter between themselves.

Poseidon: Let's have a contest to determine who shall have Athens. Let's say that whoever gives the people the finest gift will rule.

Athena: That seems fair enough. Why don't you begin?

Poseidon: This will be easy enough, for I am going to give the people a marvelous spring, bubbling with cool water.

Narrator 1: And with those words, he struck a cliff with his trident, and a spring came forth. The people of Athens gasped at its beauty, but when they tasted the water, they discovered that it was as salty as the sea Poseidon ruled.

Athena: Now it's my turn to settle this matter for eternity.

Narrator 2: Athena planted an olive tree in a tiny crevice on the rock. The people had never seen an olive tree before and marveled at its food, oil, and wood. They judged that Athena's gift was the better of the two, giving them riches forever.

Poseidon: I concede, Athena. Your gift pleases them more than mine.

Narrator 1: Athena claimed Athens as her own, and she watched over it from her temple on top of the Acropolis.

Narrator 2: With her wise and just leadership and her teaching skills, Athenians prospered, learning arts and crafts and becoming famous for their skills.

CHIRON AND ASCLEPIUS

Chiron was one of the centaurs, but he differed from this group of unruly, half-beast, half-man creatures. Chiron was kindly, and he was skilled in all manner of arts and sciences. The gods came to rely on him as a learned and just tutor, bringing him their favorite children to rear. Apollo brought Asclepius to Chiron, who raised him like a beloved son, teaching him the healing arts. Eventually, Asclepius left Chiron to heal the people of Greece. Asclepius became so skilled that he could raise the dead, incurring the wrath of Hades, god of the Underworld, who was being deprived of dead souls. Finally, Asclepius's practice of interfering with fate so angered Zeus that Zeus killed him. Apollo sought revenge by killing the Cyclopes that helped Zeus, earning Apollo a year of slavery on Earth. After being injured in a fight between the centaurs and Heracles, Chiron begged Zeus for mortality so that he could die.

Presentation

The characters can stand in the order of their speaking parts: Narrator 1, Narrator 2, Apollo, Chiron, Asclepius, Hades, and Zeus.

Props

The setting can be an outdoor setting. A mural could show a cave in the background. Chiron could wear a costume that indicates he is a centaur. Asclepius could wear robes and carry a staff that has an artificial snake wrapped around it.

Delivery Suggestions

The characters can use normal voices.

Characters

- 回 Narrator 1
- 回 Narrator 2
- 回 Apollo
- 回 Chiron
- 回 Asclepius
- 回 Hades
- 回 Zeus

CHIRON AND ASCLEPIUS

Narrator 1: Zeus suspected that Ixion, King of the Lapith people, wanted to carry off his wife, Hera. He created a cloud as a test to see if Ixion would be tempted by it. As he suspected, Ixion thought the cloud was Hera. He married it, which incurred the wrath of Zeus.

Narrator 2: This union prompted an unusual result, the birth of the first centaurs. The cloud emptied them onto the land. The centaurs were wild creatures, half man and half horse. They were vulgar and crude, living without controls of any sort.

Narrator 1: To punish Ixion, Zeus condemned him to whirl on a wheel in the Underworld for all of eternity. The centaurs were left to wreak havoc on the land, kidnapping Lapith women and trampling the crops.

Narrator 2: One centaur was different. Chiron looked like the others, but he was the son of Cronus and therefore immortal. He was a fine teacher, the greatest in all of Greece. He tutored many royal children. One day Apollo brought his son to Chiron.

Apollo: Chiron, this is my son, Asclepius.

Chiron: Good morning, Apollo and Asclepius.

Asclepius: Good morning, Chiron.

Apollo: Chiron, I would like you to raise Asclepius. He has many talents, and I want them fully developed.

Chiron: I would be honored, Apollo, but what of his mother?

Apollo: She has died. I can't raise him while tending to my other responsibilities.

Chiron: Leave him with me, Apollo. I will love him as my own.

Narrator 1: Chiron began teaching Asclepius the art of healing. He was bright and soon became very skilled. Time passed and Asclepius was ready to assert his independence.

Asclepius: Chiron, I am ready to be on my own now.

Chiron: Why? You have been like a son to me.

Asclepius: And I love you like a father, but I have learned all I can. It's time I found ways to help the people of Greece.

Chiron: Then go with my blessing.

Narrator 2: Asclepius proved to be a fine physician. People were so grateful for his help that they worshipped him as if he were a god. He carried a staff entwined with serpents, which shared secrets of medicine with him.

Narrator 1: Asclepius eventually married and had seven children. His sons became physicians, and his daughters became nurses. Hygeia, his most famous daughter, would methodically scrub her patients with soap and water, demonstrating that cleanliness was critical to recovery. The family's successes became legendary, especially when Asclepius brought the dead back to life, incurring the wrath of the gods. Hades was one of the first to complain to Zeus.

Hades: Zeus, you must do something about Asclepius!

Zeus: What is the trouble, Hades? He helps people, curing them, even saving their lives.

Hades: That's exactly the trouble. He's interfering with fate. It's been months since a soul came to me. I'm being cheated.

Zeus: That is problematic, but let's hear what Apollo has to say.

Apollo: Look at all the good he does. Surely saving a few lives isn't too much when you consider the suffering he has alleviated.

Zeus: I'll let it go for now, but I'll be watching him.

Narrator 2: Zeus kept his word, and when Asclepius accepted gold in exchange for bringing a dead person back to life, Zeus saw and lost his temper. He got a thunderbolt from one of the Cyclopes and hurled it at Asclepius, transforming him into a pile of ashes.

Narrator 1: Apollo was furious with Zeus. He couldn't seek revenge on his father, so he killed the Cyclopes who had provided the thunderbolt. Zeus called Apollo to him.

Zeus: Apollo, you have sought to hurt me by killing the Cyclopes. For punishment, you will serve as a slave on Earth for a full year.

Narrator 2: Apollo accepted his punishment and served his year with ease. Chiron, unfortunately, came to a tragic end. Although Chiron was learned and polished, the other centaurs remained crude and troublesome. During an altercation with Heracles over a jar of wine, the centaurs drew Chiron into their fight.

Narrator 1: One of Heracles's arrows hit Chiron in the knee. Heracles was immediately remorseful, for everyone knew of Chiron's fine work, but the wound would not heal. Chiron begged Zeus to let him die.

Chiron: Zeus, only you can let me go. The pain is intolerable, and I am ready for eternal rest.

Zeus: You know that I can only make you mortal if someone takes on your immortality.

Chiron: Prometheus has offered to take my place, Zeus.

Zeus: Then I will let you die, Chiron. But you will be missed among the greatest of the gods.

Narrator 2: Chiron died in his cave, and Prometheus became immortal. Even today we benefit from the teachings of the great healers, Chiron, Asclepius, and Hygeia.

DAEDALUS AND ICARUS

Born of royalty, Daedalus was a clever sculptor, architect, and inventor. After murdering his nephew, Talos, Daedalus was exiled to Crete, where he built the Labyrinth for King Minos. King Minos blamed Daedalus for the loss of his daughter Ariadne because Daedalus helped her destroy the Minotaur with Theseus, and Ariadne left thereafter. King Minos punished Daedalus and his son, Icarus, by imprisoning them in the Labyrinth. Using his ingenuity, Daedalus fashioned wings of feathers, beeswax, and string to escape. The father and son flew from prison like birds. Ignoring Daedalus's warning not to fly too high, Icarus flew too close to the sun, and the wax melted. Icarus plunged into the sea and drowned. Daedalus flew on to the island of Sicily, where he helped King Cocalus build a palace. King Minos followed in pursuit, and Daedalus killed him to avoid recapture. Icarus's story is sometimes told as a morality tale, cautioning listeners not to fly too high.

Presentation Suggestions

The narrators should stand on either side. Talos should stand to one side and exit after his lines. Daedalus should stand in the middle with King Minos on one side and King Cocalus on the other. Icarus can stand on the opposite side of Talos and exit after his lines.

Props

The kings can wear crowns. Talos, Daedalus, and Icarus can be dressed simply. Create a backdrop that shows a magnificent palace on an island with birds flying overhead. Include the sun and ocean.

Delivery Suggestions

King Minos should sound angry during most of his delivery. Talos should sound eager to please. Daedalus should sound intelligent and resourceful. King Cocalus should sound forceful and strong.

Characters

- ◙ Narrator 1
- ◙ Narrator 2
- ◙ Talos
- ◙ Daedalus
- ◙ King Minos
- ◙ Icarus
- ◙ King Cocalus

DAEDALUS AND ICARUS

Narrator 1: Daedalus was a royal Athenian, having descended from Cecrops. He was a talented artist, who loved to invent mechanical devices. For a time, he worked in Athens as a sculptor.

Narrator 2: He agreed to tutor his nephew, Talos, and found him to be an apt pupil. Talos especially enjoyed creating new things.

Talos: Daedalus, look at my latest invention. I think you'll find it clever and quite useful.

Daedalus: What is it, Talos?

Talos: I was looking at the jawbone of a serpent, and it occurred to me that it could be the model for this tool that I've designed. Give me a piece of wood, and I'll demonstrate its usefulness.

Narrator 1: Daedalus watched in amazement as Talos showed him his creation— what we now know as a saw.

Daedalus: You are clever, young Talos. This is a fine invention.

Talos: It should indeed be useful, but I have other ideas, too. Let me tell you about some of them.

Narrator 2: Secretly, Daedalus was jealous of Talos, resenting his ingenuity. Daedalus decided to get rid of Talos. They often walked together, so at the next opportunity, Daedalus threw Talos off the top of the Acropolis, ensuring that no one would be cleverer than he was.

Narrator 1: Before long, the body was discovered, and Daedalus was found guilty of murder by the court that met on Areopagus, a hill in Athens. He was sentenced to exile and fled to Crete, where he became an architect and sculptor in King Minos's court.

Narrator 2: It was there that Daedalus was asked to design the labyrinth that would house the fearsome Minotaur, which demanded annual sacrifices of seven young men and seven young women.

Narrator 1: You've heard how Theseus killed the Minotaur and later abandoned Ariadne, King Minos's daughter, on the island of Naxos. King Minos was infuriated when he discovered that his daughter Ariadne had left with the Athenians.

King Minos: Someone had to have helped Ariadne outwit the Minotaur, and there's only one person who could have done it. Daedalus designed the labyrinth, and he is the only one who knows its secrets. He shall suffer for his treachery.

Narrator 2: Daedalus was brought before King Minos, who had given great thought to an appropriate punishment. Of course, Daedalus didn't realize why King Minos had summoned him.

Daedalus: King Minos, how can I serve you?

King Minos: You have dishonored my daughter Ariadne and me. Because of you, she has fled the island with the Athenians. I have no recourse but to sentence you to the very prison you designed. You shall be taken to the labyrinth and held there. And since I have lost my daughter, your son shall also suffer. I won't banish him. I'm not that cruel. Instead, you'll have your son—but he'll be captive with you in the labyrinth. Now go!

Narrator 1: Daedalus accepted his fate, knowing that he had little choice. He resented the imposition on his son, though, and was determined to find a way out for them. He spoke to his son.

Daedalus: Icarus, I have an idea that may help us get out of here.

Icarus: Father, I knew you'd think of something. What can I do to help?

Daedalus: Collect all the feathers you can find. The birds often drop them near the entrance to the labyrinth. I'll go to the beehives nearby. With feathers, wax, and a bit of string, we can escape this underground prison.

Icarus: Father, your cleverness always amazes me. Let's get to work!

Narrator 2: Daedalus and Icarus created huge wings, made of feathers, string, and beeswax.

Icarus: How will these work, Father?

Daedalus: You've watched birds in flight, Son. The principles are the same. We'll climb out of the labyrinth and fly away. But there's one thing you must remember.

Icarus: What is that, Father?

Daedalus: The feathers are held together with beeswax. If you fly too close to the sun, it will melt, and you'll fall back to the Earth.

Icarus: Don't worry Father. I'll take care.

Narrator 1: Just as Daedalus promised, the wings worked perfectly, and together the two flew away from the labyrinth. King Minos, disgusted at their treachery, watched them leave.

King Minos: That accursed Daedalus has outwitted me again! Will I never get my vengeance?

Narrator 2: Meanwhile, Icarus was enjoying his flight. In spite of his father's warning, he kept flying higher and higher. Finally his folly sealed his fate. He flew too close to the sun. The beeswax melted, and the wings disintegrated. Daedalus could only watch helplessly as his beloved son plunged to the sea and drowned. With great sorrow, Daedalus flew on to Sicily, where King Cocalus welcomed him.

King Cocalus: Daedalus, welcome to our island. I have heard of your many skills. Do you think you can design a new palace for me? I hear that you know the procedures for installing running water.

Daedalus: I would be honored to help you in any way that I can. But we must take care in case King Minos comes searching for me.

King Cocalus: Don't worry, for you'll be under my protection. Now, let's get started!

Narrator 1: While Daedalus worked on the new palace, King Minos set off in pursuit of Daedalus in his ship. When he saw the palace construction under-way, he knew Daedalus must be involved and went to see the king of Sicily.

King Minos: King Cocalus, I am looking for Daedalus. Is he here on your island?

King Cocalus: I haven't seen him, King Minos. Perhaps he is on one of the nearby islands.

King Minos: Hmm. A shame. Well, I do have a problem that perhaps someone here can solve. I'll leave you this conch shell. I am looking for someone who could pull a thread through its windings. I'll give a sack of gold as a reward.

King Cocalus: An interesting challenge. Let me see what I can do to solve it.

Narrator 2: Attracted by the potential reward, King Cocalus asked Daedalus if he could meet the challenge.

Daedalus: Here's what we'll do. Tie the thread on this ant. Then put a bit of honey at the other end of the shell. Watch what happens.

Narrator 1: When King Minos saw the ant pull the thread through the shell, he knew that only one person could have been so clever as to meet this challenge.

King Minos: There is only one man who could do this. Bring Daedalus to me!

Narrator 2: The Sicilian king had no choice, but he knew Daedalus wouldn't come willingly. He stalled for time, pretending to cooperate with King Minos.

King Cocalus: I will have to dupe Daedalus into coming here. I'm having a feast tonight. Why don't you join us, and you can capture him there. Meanwhile, would you like to bathe after your long journey? My palace is equipped with running water.

King Minos: A good plan! And yes, I would appreciate a bath.

Narrator 1: King Cocalus called for Daedalus so that he could warn him.

King Cocalus: Daedalus, King Minos has caught up with you and demanded I release you to him. I have convinced him that you can be captured at tonight's feast. It's up to you to determine your fate.

Daedalus: Will King Minos bathe before the feast?

King Cocalus: Yes, I extended the invitation to him to use the new baths you have installed.

Daedalus: Then you needn't worry. I'll take care of him.

Narrator 2: As King Minos prepared for his bath, Daedalus made his own preparations. When King Minos stepped into the bath and turned on the tap, boiling water rushed out of the tap, scalding him to death.

Narrator 1: Free of his enemy, Daedalus spent the rest of his life serving the King of Sicily.

DEMETER
AND
PERSEPHONE

The name Demeter means "barley mother." The goddess of agriculture, her Latin name, Ceres, inspired the word *cereal.* Persephone, also known as Kore (Proserpina in Latin), was born to Demeter but was abducted by Hades and taken to the Underworld. Demeter disguised herself as an old woman and wandered the world, searching for Persephone. During her travels, she was befriended by Metaneira, who retained Demeter to care for her infant son. When Metaneira suspected Demeter of harming her son, Demeter explained that she was a goddess. She gave Metaneira's elder son Triptolemus the gift of corn and a winged chariot to distribute it. After more searching, Demeter returned to her throne and decreed that the earth would become barren. Zeus intervened, forcing Hades to return Persephone. Unfortunately, Persephone had eaten the forbidden pomegranate seeds, and this forever linked her to the Underworld. Knowing that Demeter would continue to make mortals suffer, Zeus struck a compromise, sending Persephone to the Underworld for part of each year in what has come to be known as the winter season.

Presentation Suggestions

The narrators can stand on opposite sides of the stage. Demeter should stand in the center with Hades and Persephone seated in chairs in front of her. Metaneira and Triptolemus should be on one side of Demeter, with Zeus and Iris on the other side.

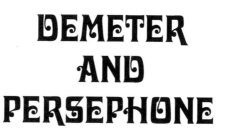

Props

The stage could be decorated with corn stalks, flowers, and plants to represent Demeter's role as the goddess of agriculture. Hades should be dressed in dark, menacing clothing. Persephone and Demeter should be dressed in colorful or flowery clothes. Demeter could slip a dark robe over her clothes when disguised as the old woman. Metaneira and Triptolemus can be dressed in regular clothes, with Zeus and Iris in more regal clothing.

Delivery Suggestions

The characters should adapt their voices to suit the story, varying the delivery as the story progresses.

Characters

▣ Narrator 1
▣ Narrator 2
▣ Hades
▣ Demeter
▣ Persephone
▣ Metaneira
▣ Triptolemus
▣ Zeus
▣ Iris

DEMETER AND PERSEPHONE

Narrator 1: Persephone was the beloved daughter of Demeter, the goddess of the harvest. When Demeter sat on her throne, Persephone played on her lap, and Demeter always took Persephone along on her trips to Earth to watch over the crops.

Narrator 2: Persephone danced through life, enjoying every moment. She was such a delightful youngster that flowers would spring up under her feet. Everyone noticed her, appreciating her beauty and joy. Unfortunately, even Hades, god of the Underworld, who rarely noticed anything outside of his domain, watched the young beauty, falling in love with her grace and spirit. Hades vowed to have her for himself.

Hades: Persephone is indeed a rare young beauty, worthy of being my queen. I know her mother will never let me marry her, so I will simply have to watch for the chance to kidnap her.

Narrator 1: Before long, Hades saw that opportunity unfold.

Demeter: Persephone, play with the nymphs in the field for a while. While you play, gather some flowers that we can take home.

Persephone: I'll make a huge bouquet just for you, Mother!

Demeter: Just remember not to wander off by yourself, daughter.

Persephone: Don't worry, Mother. I have the nymphs to play with.

Narrator 2: But Persephone became so enchanted by the lovely flowers that she wandered away from the nymphs, giving Hades the opportunity he wanted.

Hades: There she is, just above my reach. I'll simply split open the ground, grab Persephone, and take her back to the Underworld with me. She'll adjust to her new life as my queen soon enough.

Narrator 1: Driving his dark chariot and black horses through a crevice in the Earth, Hades captured Persephone. Soon Demeter began to call for her.

Demeter: Persephone, where are you? Come and bring the flowers now.

Narrator 2: Demeter couldn't find Persephone, who had vanished from the meadow. Demeter had no idea that Hades was driving his chariot back to the Underworld, clutching the frightened child as he drove.

Persephone: Where are you taking me?

Hades: To my home, my dear, where you'll be crowned with gold and precious stones.

Persephone: But I don't want to go with you! I want to stay with my mother!

Hades: You'll forget about her in no time, Persephone.

Narrator 1: Hades seated her beside him on the throne, but Persephone was inconsolable. She cared nothing for the gold and jewels, wanting only to see the sun, flowers, and her beloved mother.

Narrator 2: Dead spirits crept out from their hiding places to see the new queen, but Persephone had no interest in their tortured souls. Hades encouraged her to appreciate his gloomy world.

Hades: Persephone, you must come see my garden. Perhaps it will lift your spirits.

Narrator 1: But Persephone found no joy in a garden of weeping willows and whispering poplars.

Persephone: This is hardly a garden. Where are the birds, the fruit, and the flowers?

Hades: Ah, but there is fruit here, the pomegranate. Come and have a taste from the pomegranate tree.

Narrator 2: Persephone knew that she shouldn't eat of the food of the dead, but she longed to try the pomegranate and ate two seeds. Meanwhile, Demeter continued to search for her daughter. Wandering the world in the guise of an old woman. She came to the home of Metaneira, the wife of Celeüs, and their newborn son Demophon. Metaneira recognized Demeter's grace and treated her with great respect.

Metaneira: You are welcome in our home and to our food and drink. Won't you join us for our meal?

Narrator 1: Demeter remained quiet, but she transferred her grief for her missing daughter to love for the young Demophon. Metaneira noticed her devotion to the child and decided to entrust his care to Demeter.

Metaneira: I see that you love babies. Would you like to care for Demophon?

Narrator 2: Demeter nodded and settled in to care for him with great devotion. Becoming quite fond of him, she decided to transform him into a god to ensure his immortality. Each night she anointed him with ambrosia, then hid him in the fire to destroy his mortal nature. The infant began to grow like a god, but Metaneira became suspicious and spied on Demeter, catching her as she put him in the fire.

Metaneira: What are you doing to my son? I'm taking him out now!

Demeter: You foolish woman! By taking him from the fire, you've doomed him to the life of mortals. I would have ensured that he would live forever as a god!

Metaneira: Who are you? How do you have these powers?

Demeter: I came to you in disguise, and I am truly Demeter. I know you think I have betrayed your trust, but I haven't, and I want to show my appreciation for your kindness. Bring Triptolemus to me.

Narrator 1: Metaneira believed Demeter, and sent for her oldest son, Triptolemus, who came at his mother's bidding.

Demeter: Triptolemus, I am giving you great gifts that will benefit both you and your people. Take these grains of corn, a most precious form of sustenance.

Triptolemus: Thank you, but what do I do with it?

Demeter: I will show you how to use a plough and how to harness oxen to do the hard work.

Triptolemus: What do I do after I have ploughed the fields?

Demeter: Sow the field with these grains and tend it with water. In time, corn will grow, which you may eat, but you must always save some grains for the next year.

Triptolemus: This will be a wonderful gift, and I will always be grateful for your generosity.

Demeter: There is one more gift, Triptolemus. I am giving you this winged chariot and these fine dragons to help you spread the grain across your earth. And now I bid you leave, as I must continue on my journey.

Narrator 2: Demeter continued to roam the Earth, giving gifts such as the olive tree. The Earth benefited from the gift of grain and the olive tree, but finally she returned to her temple at Eleusis and prepared to exact her revenge.

Demeter: I have searched throughout the world for my precious daughter, and no one has stepped forward to help me in my quest. No longer will I be the kind goddess helping the crops prosper so that bellies can be full and satisfied. From this day forward, the Earth is forbidden to produce any crops!

Narrator 1: With that heartless pronouncement, the Earth entered a cruel period of drought and devastation. The entire human race would have perished of relentless hunger if Zeus hadn't intervened.

Zeus: Iris, go to Demeter and try to convince her to change her mind.

Narrator 2: Iris went immediately to see Demeter.

Iris: Demeter, Zeus sends me to you, beseeching you to reconsider. The mortals are starving, and you alone can restore bounty to the Earth.

Demeter: Return to Zeus and tell him that until I have Persephone safely home, the Earth and all its inhabitants will suffer as I have suffered.

Narrator 1: Iris returned to Zeus with great haste.

Iris: Zeus, I bring distressing news. Demeter is determined to stay with her plan of revenge and refuses to reverse her directive.

Zeus: Thank you for trying, Iris. Send Hermes to me so that I can put pressure on Hades to return Persephone to Demeter.

Narrator 2: Hades agreed to return Persephone, but he knew that by eating the pomegranate, she would be forever bound to him. The reunion with Demeter was joyful at first.

Demeter: Persephone, what a relief to have you home with me. But I hope you remembered not to eat anything while in the Underworld.

Persephone: I'm sorry, Mother, but I couldn't resist tasting the pomegranate seeds. I missed fruit so much and had so little to enjoy there.

Demeter: My dear, you are lost to me again unless we can convince Zeus to intervene.

Narrator 1: Demeter took Persephone to see Zeus, explained the situation, and begged him to find a solution.

Zeus: You know that once Persephone ate the pomegranate seeds, she was bound to Hades forever. Still, I can't face another devastating year for the mortals. She will be allowed to spend most of her life with the gods, but for three months each year, she must return to the Underworld to fulfill her obligation to Hades.

Narrator 2: Demeter knew that Zeus had found a fair compromise, but she continued to grieve each winter when Persephone returned to the Underworld. This explains why, to this very day, there is a gray period of mourning each year when flowers, seeds, trees, and all that gives life sleeps until Persephone returns from the Underworld.

DEUCALION AND PYRRHA

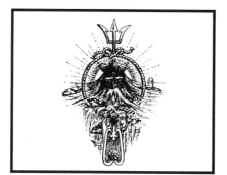

Deucalion, the son of Prometheus, often visited his father to help him cope with the relentless torture of the eagle. Prometheus warned him that Zeus planned to flood the Earth, urging him to build an ark. Deucalion's wife, Pyrrha, the daughter of Epimetheus and Pandora, was a devout woman and dedicated wife to Deucalion. They built the ark, surviving the nine days and nights of the flood. Unlike the events in the Noah story, they alone survive the flood. After landing on Mount Parnassus, they restored a temple that was covered in seaweed. After offering their thanks for surviving to the gods, Zeus took pity on them, granting them the opportunity to repopulate the Earth.

Presentation Suggestions

Consider presenting this after "Prometheus and Pandora," perhaps using the same people for the common characters. Because there are only six characters, they should stay on stage throughout the reading. The characters should be placed in the following order: Narrator 1, Narrator 2, Prometheus, Deucalion, Pyrrha, and Zeus. Deucalion and Pyrrha should stand slightly in front of the other readers.

Props

This script provides an opportunity to use a nautical theme. Create a backdrop with a mural of an ark, showing Mount Parnassus in the distance. Decorate the stage with netting, fishes, and the like. Zeus should be dressed regally, while the other characters can be dressed in simple clothing.

Delivery Suggestions

All readers should use normal voices.

Characters

- 🔲 Narrator 1
- 🔲 Narrator 2
- 🔲 Prometheus
- 🔲 Deucalion
- 🔲 Pyrrha
- 🔲 Zeus

DEUCALION AND PYRRHA

Narrator 1: Deucalion, the son of Prometheus, often went to visit his father, who spent many years chained to the top of the Caucasus Mountains. Prometheus had angered Zeus by giving mortals the gift of fire and teaching them how to prepare meat. Once the mortals learned to cook meat, they kept the best portions for themselves.

Narrator 2: Deucalion couldn't save Prometheus from Zeus's wrath, but while he visited his father, he could at least keep away the eagle that continually tortured Prometheus.

Narrator 1: Prometheus had the gift of prophecy, and he knew that although Zeus had sent Pandora to Earth to unleash an eternity of miseries on mortals, he still wanted revenge. Prometheus desperately wanted to save his son.

Prometheus: Deucalion, Zeus is going to punish all the creatures that live on Earth.

Deucalion: What can I do, Father? Is there any way to stop him?

Prometheus: There's no stopping Zeus, I fear. I can see a great flood coming. But there may be a way to at least save you and your wife. Can you trust my guidance?

Deucalion: Of course, Father, just tell me what to do.

Prometheus: Build an ark, making it as sturdy as you can. But you must work quickly; I'm not sure how much time you have. Be sure that you have adequate provisions for you and your wife. Don't forget to take embers with you so fire won't be lost to you.

Deucalion: As you wish, Father.

Narrator 2: Deucalion's wife was the first woman on Earth, born to Epimetheus and Pandora. Deucalion explained the daunting task ahead as they talked quietly together.

Deucalion: Pyrrha, I come from my visit with my father, and he sees a great flood coming. We need to prepare by building an ark. We can save ourselves, but only if we hurry.

Pyrrha: Your father has never been wrong in his prophecies. Let's waste no more time and begin building the ark.

Narrator 1: Deucalion and Pyrrha worked side by side. As they finished stocking the ark with food, the wind picked up, and raindrops splashed onto their heads. As they huddled on the deck, the heavens opened, and a torrent of rain poured forth.

Pyrrha: Prometheus was right, I fear. Let's go inside where we'll be safe, my husband.

Narrator 2: The rain relentlessly beat upon the ark, but Deucalion and Pyrrha stayed safe and dry as the ark began to rise with the floodwaters. Although it was hard to tell day from night, Deucalion knew that much time had passed.

Deucalion: Pyrrha, this is the ninth night of rain. How much longer can this continue?

Pyrrha: Zeus is a vengeful god, Deucalion. We were fortunate that Prometheus saw the future accurately. Let's be patient. Surely Zeus will tire of this rain.

Narrator 1: The next morning, the rain began to lessen. Pyrrha and Deucalion stood on the deck of the ark, looking about in amazement.

Deucalion: Pyrrha, look at this vast sea! I wonder if the waters will recede enough for us to ever see land again.

Pyrrha: Over there, Deucalion! It looks like a mountain in the distance.

Narrator 2: As the sun began to break through the clouds, Deucalion and Pyrrha could see the top of Mount Parnassus. The only other mountain peak above the floodwaters was Mount Olympus, the home of the gods.

Narrator 1: The ark drifted slowly toward Mount Parnassus, and soon Deucalion and Pyrrha stepped from the ark to search for signs of any survivors.

Deucalion: Pyrrha, I'm afraid Zeus has succeeded once again. How could any mortal survive this deluge?

Pyrrha: Let's continue searching, Deucalion. I see a temple in the distance. Perhaps we'll find something there.

Narrator 2: But when they arrived at the temple, all they found were remnants of the flood—seaweed and dead sea creatures lost when the waters receded.

Deucalion: The sea doused the sacred fire. Let's return to the ark and get one of the embers so we can light the fire again.

Pyrrha: I'll go, my husband, while you stay and begin restoring the temple as best you can. Once we light the fire again, we can say our prayers of thanks to the gods for staying alive through the flood.

Narrator 1: And thus they cleaned up the temple, lit the fire, and gave thanks to the gods. Zeus looked down on them and felt sorry for their loneliness. He spoke to them from the top of Mount Olympus.

Zeus: Deucalion, Pyrrha, listen to me.

Deucalion: What is it, Zeus?

Zeus: I'm impressed by your ingenuity in building the ark and by your piety in restoring the temple. I'll grant you one wish. What will it be?

Deucalion: We are grateful to be alive, but we are lonely.

Pyrrha: If we are indeed the only survivors of the flood, could you create some companions for us?

Zeus: You will do this yourselves. Cover your heads with veils and then pick up the bones of your mother and throw them over your shoulders.

Pyrrha: We have no mother. Everyone has perished in the flood.

Deucalion: I know what he means, Pyrrha. He doesn't mean your mortal mother. He speaks of the bones of our Mother Earth. Let's do as he says. Cover your head and then pick up a handful of stones and throw them over your shoulder.

Narrator 2: As they threw the stones, a new line of mortals sprang up. Behind Deucalion appeared a score of men and behind Pyrrha, twenty women. These mortals, having come from stone, were much hardier than those fashioned of clay by Prometheus and Epithemeus. The new mortals were able to withstand the torment of the miseries unleashed by Pandora, those miseries having flown above the Earth to escape the floodwaters.

Narrator 1: Zeus allowed the new race, often called Deucalion's race, to prosper. Deucalion became an important king, founding towns and building temples. Legend has it that Deucalion and Pyrrha had long lives and many descendants.

DIONYSUS

Dionysus is also called Bacchus, and his name means "lame deity." He is best known as the god of wine, but his place in mythology broadened over the years, and he later became known as the god of vegetation, fruitfulness, theater, pleasures, and civilization. Son of Zeus, he was the only one of the twelve great gods whose mother was a mortal. Dionysus was nearly lost to Zeus when Hera convinced Semele, Dionysus's mother, that Zeus should show himself as a true god. His brilliance in his true form caused Semele to catch fire, almost destroying the unborn child. Zeus saved the infant, then he offered his protection repeatedly as Hera tried time and again to destroy Dionysus. During his wanderings, Dionysus discovered grapes and how to make wine. Eventually he rescued and married Adriane, returning to Olympus where Zeus welcomed him in the great hall.

Presentation Suggestions

Narrator 1 should sit on a stool, with Narrator 2 sitting on a chair in front of Narrator 1. Hera, Semele, Zeus, and Hermes should be on one side, in order of their speaking. Dionysus should be in the center. Dodona should be on the side opposite the other characters but can leave the stage after his lines. The pirates can come on stage for their part, replacing Dodona. Ariadne can enter for her lines, remaining on stage for the conclusion.

Props

The stage could be decorated with clusters of grapes, greenery, and earthenware jugs. The gods could be dressed in regal clothing. Dionysus can be dressed simply but elegantly. Dodona should look wise, perhaps dressed in flowing robes. The pirates could have mock cutlasses and be dressed in rough clothing.

Delivery

The characters generally should use normal voices. Hera should sound persuasive when dealing with Semele. Zeus should sound determined to save Dionysus. Dionysus should sound young. Dodona should sound wise. Pirate 1 and Pirate 2 should sound greedy and ruthless, and Pirate 3 should sound concerned and cautious.

Characters

- ◙ Narrator 1
- ◙ Narrator 2
- ◙ Hera
- ◙ Semele
- ◙ Zeus
- ◙ Hermes
- ◙ Dionysus
- ◙ Dodona
- ◙ Pirate 1
- ◙ Pirate 2
- ◙ Pirate 3
- ◙ Ariadne

DIONYSUS

Narrator 1: Although Zeus was a most powerful god, he never knew when Hera's jealousy would make mischief. Zeus had become enchanted with the princess Semele, the mortal daughter of the King of Thebes. Of course Hera discovered that, once again, Zeus had given in to the temptations of a beautiful woman.

Narrator 2: Hera became infuriated when she learned that Semele was expecting Zeus's child. She disguised herself as an old nurse and went to visit Semele, making small talk to disarm her.

Hera: Good day, Semele. What a lovely palace your father has provided. And I see that you are to be blessed with a child.

Semele: Good day to you. I'm sorry that I don't recall meeting you before. Have we met?

Hera: We've met at the baths, but I'm just a forgettable old woman.

Semele: I doubt that you are forgettable, and I'm glad to become acquainted with you.

Hera: Is your husband at home?

Semele: No, his duties keep him away often.

Hera: Just what does he do?

Semele: He's the mighty Zeus, the god of creation.

Hera: Really? Do you think he's telling you the truth? Many husbands claim to be gods, but few live up to their claims.

Semele: I have no reason to doubt my husband.

Hera: I'm sure you know him well, but if I were you, I'd want to see just how mighty he truly is. I'd ask him to show himself as a god.

Semele: I'll give your words some thought, but now I must rest. Being with child leaves me weary.

Narrator 1: Semele tried to forget about the old woman's comments, but they nagged at her like a pesky fly. Finally, when Zeus came to see her in mortal form, she couldn't ignore her suspicions. She decided to put him to the test.

Semele: Would you grant me any wish, my dear?

Zeus: Of course, Semele. Just name what your heart desires.

Semele: Do you swear to grant me your wish?

Zeus: I swear by the River Styx!

Semele: You say you are a god, but I have little evidence to prove what you claim. Show yourself as you truly are.

Zeus: Semele, that would be disastrous. No mortal can look upon me and survive. Ask anything else of me, but not that.

Semele: But that is the only wish I have—and you gave your solemn oath.

Zeus: My dear, I will fulfill your request, but know that I wish you had never asked for it.

Narrator 2: With those words, Zeus showed himself as the mighty god of thunder, hoping Semele could survive. But he was so brilliant that she instantly caught fire and died.

Narrator 1: Zeus moved quickly and plucked Semele's child from her womb. He sewed him into his thigh and returned to the heavens. Once the child had matured, he took him out, planning how to conceal the babe from Hera. He called Hermes to his throne.

Hermes: Your majesty, how can I serve you?

Zeus: There is a babe who I need hidden away. His name is Dionysus, and it is imperative that Hera not discover him.

Hermes: What about King Athamas and his wife Ino? They would be good parents and can be trusted.

Zeus: Yes, they are a good choice. Take the babe now. Explain to them that he is my son and that I want him to be treated with respect and care.

Hermes: Of course. Trust that he'll be well cared for. I'll keep an eye on him as well.

Narrator 2: Hermes carried the child to King Athamas and Ino. They dressed him as a girl to try to deceive Hera, but she discerned the truth. She used her powers to turn Ino mad, and Zeus had to once again rescue Dionysus. Again he summoned Hermes for help.

Zeus: Hermes, Hera has struck again, and I need you to take Dionysus far away.

Hermes: Do you have any ideas where he'll be safe?

Zeus: I've changed him into a kid for safekeeping. Deliver him to the nymphs in the valley of Nysa. He should be safe there.

Hermes: I'll take him there immediately.

Narrator 1: The nymphs welcomed Dionysus, and he grew up on the mountain of Nysa, playing among leopards and tigers. The muses helped with his upbringing as well. As he grew to manhood, he wandered the valley with the nymphs, discovering grapes and the art of making wine.

Narrator 2: But once again Hera disrupted Dionysus's idyllic life. She discovered that he was still alive and plotted her vengeance. She decided to make Dionysus suffer like Ino, turning him mad.

Narrator 1: But Dionysus was wise enough to realize that he needed help. He sought out Dodona, the oracle.

Dionysus: Dodona, I come beseeching you to help me with my affliction.

Dodona: What is the problem, my son?

Dionysus: I have been struck with madness.

Dodona: I can help you, but then you must follow my directives.

Dionysus: Just tell me what to do, as long as I can think clearly again.

Dodona: You'll soon feel whole, Dionysus. Then you should continue your travels. Take what you know about creating wine to the world. Go on long journeys, share your knowledge, and you'll have grand adventures.

Narrator 2: Dionysus listened well to Dodona and had many exciting escapades. One of his grandest occurred as he was traveling from island to island. He was sleeping on a beach when a band of pirates sailed by. They spied him, plotting his capture and ransom.

Pirate 1: Look at that youth. He must be a prince, yet he lies sleeping as if nearly dead.

Pirate 2: Let's take him with us! He'll fetch a handsome reward, and if he doesn't we can dispose of him easily enough.

Narrator 1: The pirates collected Dionysus without him ever waking up. One of the other pirates wasn't convinced that this kidnapping was wise.

Pirate 3: Look at his features. He is not just a prince, but probably a god. I think we're making a mistake.

Pirate 1: Don't be foolish. What god would hide in such a youth? He is entirely too pretty.

Pirate 2: You worry too much. Let's be off and worry about him later. He looks like he has drunk so much wine that he'll be sleeping it off for hours.

Narrator 2: Dionysus did sleep deeply, but soon the movement of the ship woke him.

Dionysus: Where am I? How did I get on this ship? Where are you taking me?

Pirate 3: Don't worry. Just tell us where you want to go, and we'll take you home.

Dionysus: Then take me to Naxos, for that is my home.

Narrator 1: But the other pirates headed away from Naxos.

Dionysus: This is the wrong direction. Turn the ship!

Pirate 1: Sorry to disappoint you, but we have other plans for you.

Pirate 2: That's right. You're far too valuable a cargo to just return without payment.

Dionysus: You'll regret this. Turn the ship now!

Narrator 2: The men ignored him. Suddenly the ship stood still.

Pirate 1: What has happened to the wind?

Pirate 2: This can't be happening! Man the oars! Row, men!

Pirate 3: I told you that he was a god. You're making a grave mistake.

Pirate 1: It's too late to argue! Help us row!

Narrator 1: In spite of their Herculean efforts, the ship stood still. Soon ivy covered their oars. Vines with huge clumps of fruit hung from the mast. Dionysus stood in the middle of the ship, with tigers, lynxes, and panthers pacing restlessly around him. Wine flowed across the decks of the ship.

Narrator 2: Dionysus looked at all of the pirates except for the one who defended him. As he stared, each one in turn shrank to mere inches. Their arms became fins, their feet became tails, their skin transformed into scales, and their faces turned into fish mouths. They frantically floundered across the deck and lurched into the sea. One pirate remained.

Pirate 3: How can I serve you, my lord?

Dionysus: Do not fear me, but take me to Naxos. I will help you steer the ship.

Narrator 1: And so they sailed on to Naxos, where Dionysus ensured that the faithful pirate would retain the ship and have a life of riches.

Narrator 2: While on the isle of Naxos, Dionysus came upon a young woman, sleeping on the shore, much as he had when he was captured. This was Ariadne, whom Theseus had just abandoned. Ariadne woke, distressed to find herself with a stranger.

Ariadne: Where is Theseus? Who are you?

Dionysus: I am Dionysus, and I found you alone, sleeping soundly. As for Theseus, could that be his ship that I see on the horizon?

Ariadne: That scoundrel! He has left me here with no resources! What am I to do?

Dionysus: You have no need to worry. Tell me your name, and how you came to be betrayed.

Ariadne: I am Ariadne, daughter of Minos and Pasiphaë. I fell in love with Theseus and helped him fight the Minotaur in Crete. He would have been lost in the labyrinth but for the ball of thread I gave him. We escaped to this island, but now he has shown his true self.

Dionysus: Come with me, and I'll protect you. Forget about this worthless scoundrel.

Narrator 1: Ariadne appreciated the young god's kindness and soon fell in love with him. They married, and Dionysus carried her off to dwell among the gods of Olympus. Dionysus's arrival stirred Hera to anger once again.

Hera: I refuse to have the son of a mortal sitting in our royal hall.

Zeus: Hera, you have caused enough mischief! Dionysus stays!

Narrator 2: Dionysus went to Zeus with a request.

Dionysus: Before I take the throne, I wish to see my mother.

Zeus: Yes, it is time that some wrongs are made right. I'll give you safe passage to Hades. Then you must convince Hades to release your mother.

Narrator 1: Hades agreed to release Semele if Dionysus would give up something he loved. He agreed, giving up the myrtle. Dionysus ascended to Olympus, where he was honored for his gifts of wine and fruit. Zeus rewarded the nymphs for raising Dionysus by making them stars in the constellation of the Hyades. Dionysus enjoyed many years of glory and merriment.

EOS, SELENE, AND HELIOS

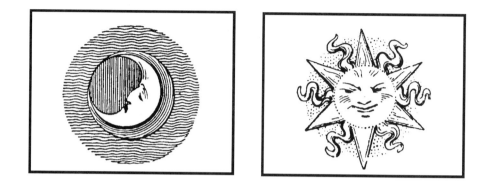

Eos, Selene, and Helios, the dawn, moon, and sun, dominated the sky. Eos began each day by summoning forth the dawn. Helios, known as Apollo in later myths, would drive his chariot across the sky, bringing forth the sun. Selene drove her silver chariot across the sky at night. Eos fell in love with a young man, asking Zeus to let him live forever. Eos's husband lived forever, but he continued to age until he had shrunk to a cricket. Selene also fell in love with a mortal but asked that Zeus have him sleep eternally so that she could visit him nightly. Helios's son begged him to be allowed to drive the chariot across the sky. Finally, Helios gave in, but the horses sensed untrained hands at the reins and rampaged across the sky. To stop the chaos, Zeus struck the chariot with a thunderbolt, and Phaëthon plunged to his death.

Presentation Suggestions

Arrange the characters in the following order: Narrator 1, Narrator 2, Eos, Selene, Helios, Phaëthon, and Zeus.

Props

Decorate the stage with a backdrop showing the moon and stars high in the sky and the dawn just coming up. Eos can dress in pink to represent the pink dawn. Selene can be dressed in silver. Helios can wear bright yellow.

Delivery Suggestions

Phaëthon should sound persuasive and demanding as he convinces Helios to let him drive the chariot. Generally, the characters should read in normal voices.

Characters

- ◙ Narrator 1
- ◙ Eos
- ◙ Narrator 2
- ◙ Zeus
- ◙ Selene
- ◙ Phaëthon
- ◙ Helios

EOS, SELENE, AND HELIOS

Narrator 1: The mortals could greet a new day because Eos, the dawn, rose without fail to announce each morning. Daughter of Hyperion and Theia, she was mother to the four winds, Boreas, Zephyrus, Notus, and Eurus.

Eos: Another beautiful day has arrived! Wake up, trees! Men and women, rejoice in the coming sunshine! And all you beasts, stretch out and greet the day.

Narrator 2: Eos would sprinkle dew over the grass and flowers as everything living woke to a bright new day. Eos had many loves during her lifetime, but a favorite was a mortal. One morning, Eos saw a young prince waking up. Tithonus, the son of Laomedon, entranced Eos.

Eos: What a handsome young prince! He is perfect! I'll just visit Zeus and see if I can't have him for myself.

Narrator 1: After starting a new day, Eos went to see Zeus.

Eos: Kind Zeus, I have a request for you.

Zeus: What would you like, Eos?

Eos: There is a young prince named Tithonus. He pleases me, and I would like to marry him.

Zeus: But he is mortal, Eos.

Eos: You could grant him eternal life. Would you do that for me, Zeus? Only he will make me happy.

Zeus: You have been faithful in your daily endeavors. Of course, I'll grant eternal life to Tithonus if that will make you happy.

Narrator 2: Eos took Tithonus to Ethiopia, where they enjoyed their lives together for many years. They had two sons, Emathion and Memnon. Emathion ruled over Arabia, and Memnon reigned over Ethiopia for years. Eos was proud of her sons.

Narrator 1: After a number of years, Eos realized that Tithonus was aging. Although she had requested eternal life for him, she hadn't thought to ask for eternal youth. Tithonus began to show his age. He shrank, becoming feeble and frail. Finally, Eos was so ashamed of him that she kept him hidden in the palace. While Eos stayed eternally young, Tithonus shrank until he became a cricket, destined to chirp helplessly forever.

Narrator 2: Eos had a sister, Selene, the moon, who only came out at night, driving her white horses and silver chariot gently across the sky. One night Selene's soft moonbeams fell on Endymion, a young shepherd.

Narrator 1: Selene fell instantly in love with the handsome youth, just as Eos had fallen in love with Tithonus. But Selene had learned a lesson from her sister's experience with asking Zeus to have a mortal.

Selene: Zeus, I have found a youth whom I love. I can't bear to lose him to another suitor.

Zeus: What do you want, Selene?

Selene: As long as he sleeps, no one else can have him except me. I'll be able to visit him every night.

Zeus: Are you certain this is what you want, Selene? Think this through carefully.

Selene: Yes, Zeus. He'll be mine, sleeping peacefully through eternity.

Narrator 2: Every night, Selene visited the youth while he slept. Endymion smiled in his sleep and always looked handsome.

Narrator 1: And every night, smiling sweetly, he dreamed he held the moon in his arms.

Narrator 2: Eos continued to bring dawn to the world, welcoming Helios, the sun, who drove his glowing chariot across the sky every day. He was so brilliant that only the gods could look at him. Mortals would become blind if they dared look at his fiery light.

Narrator 1: Helios had five daughters, the Heliades, who unharnessed the horse every night at the end of Helios's journeys. His son, Phaëthon, pestered Helios with a request.

Phaëthon: Father, when can I drive the chariot across the sky and bring light to all the Earth and sky?

Helios: Son, that is a grave responsibility. The route must be maintained at all costs, or destruction may befall everyone in the heavens above and on the Earth below.

Phaëthon: Please, Father, I'm grown now. Haven't you seen how responsible I've become? It's time you shared the work with me. Let me prove to you that I have earned the right to be called your son.

Helios: You wage a convincing argument, but you must heed my admonitions and only follow the route that has been followed for all of time. And the horses, Son, they are difficult to handle. Are you certain you are ready to do this?

Phaëthon: Of course, Father. I only need to drive it once. Then you'll see that I can handle the horses and keep to the route.

Helios: I'll let you drive them when Eos comes again. I hope I don't regret this.

Narrator 2: Before Phaëthon departed the next morning, Helios put a special ointment on him so that the sun wouldn't burn his skin.

Helios: Son, remember to follow the true path. Don't fly too close to the sun or the stars, and keep the horses under control.

Phaëthon: Of course, Father. Trust me, I'll make you proud.

Narrator 1: Phaëthon meant well, and at first he kept to the course while keeping the horses in check. But the horses began to realize that unskilled hands were at the reins. They began to speed toward the constellations, enraging the animals of the zodiac.

Narrator 2: The lion roared, and the bull charged. The horses reared, throwing Phaëthon nearly out of the chariot. The horses continued on their reckless course. They dipped down to the Earth, scorching the ground with the chariot's heat. Then they flew so high that the Earth below froze and was covered with ice.

Zeus: This is disastrous! Why Helios let that youngster drive his chariot is beyond my understanding. I'll have to stop the chariot now.

Narrator 1: Zeus threw a thunderbolt at the chariot, dashing it to the ground. Phaëthon plunged into the river and died. Helios was so grief stricken that Hephaestus, god of fire and metalworking, had to work through the night to repair his chariot, or Helios would not be able to bring the sun in the morning. But Helios had learned his lesson. No one but he would ever drive the chariot again.

EROS AND PSYCHE

The term *psyche* is Greek for "soul." Born to a family of three beautiful sisters, Psyche's beauty was almost as legendary as that of Helen. An oracle predicted that she would marry a "monster," and jealous Aphrodite insisted that Eros carry out this prediction. But Eros intervened, falling in love with Psyche and hiding her in a palace. He visited Psyche only at night, forbidding her to look on him. Psyche eventually became discontent with never seeing her husband during his nocturnal visits, and she lit a lamp to peek at his sleeping form. A drop of oil fell on him, he woke up, and quickly departed, leaving Psyche alone. Psyche wandered the world searching for him until the gods took pity on her. According to Ernest Crawley (*The Mystic Rose,* New York: Meridian Books, 1960, p. 42), the story probably arose from the custom in ancient Sparta of young husbands only visiting their wives at night. In the familiar Latin version, Venus is the jealous goddess, inadvertently sending her son Cupid to Psyche's side.

Presentation Suggestions

Eros and Psyche can sit on stools in the center of the stage. The narrators and sisters can stand on one side of the stage. Father, the Oracle, and Aphrodite can stand on the other side of the stage.

Props

Psyche and Eros can be dressed in simple, elegant clothing. Eros can have a bow and arrows nearby. Father can be dressed like royalty. The oracle should be in simple clothing. Aphrodite should be in a long, flowing gown. The sisters should wear dresses.

Delivery Suggestions

Eros should sound kind and persuasive. Psyche should sound somewhat evasive when describing her unusual marital arrangement to her sisters and desperate when she loses Eros. The sisters should sound skeptical about Psyche's trust in her husband.

Characters

- ◙ Narrator 1
- ◙ Father
- ◙ Oracle
- ◙ Narrator 2
- ◙ Aphrodite
- ◙ Eros
- ◙ Psyche
- ◙ Sister 1
- ◙ Sister 2

EROS AND PSYCHE

Narrator 1: Once there was a king who had three beautiful daughters. People came from distant lands just to gaze upon these three exquisite creatures, especially the one called Psyche. Soon Psyche's sisters were married, but Psyche's beauty was so stunning that she intimidated all who dared even to think of marrying her. Her father was unsure of how he should direct her future and consulted an oracle.

Father: I have come here seeking your wisdom about my daughter.

Oracle: Tell me about her.

Father: She is an exquisite young woman, but she is so beautiful that men are afraid of her. It's time that she marry, but men take one look at her and fear they could never win her heart.

Oracle: Your daughter is indeed beautiful, and she will marry. But she will marry a horrible monster.

Father: How can this be? She is a delicate young woman who has done no harm to man or beast. Surely this fate is unworthy and cruel.

Oracle: You came to me to learn what to do, and you know that you can't escape what the Fates have prophesied.

Father: What must I do?

Oracle: Dress her to be married and take her to the summit of the mountain. There she will be claimed.

Narrator 2: Psyche's distraught father returned home, wondering how he would find the words to explain to his wife and daughter what lay ahead. Soon, with heavy hearts, Psyche's parents dressed her in wedding clothes and led her to the mountain, where they explained her fate to their daughter and tearfully bade her good-bye.

Narrator 1: In truth, as often happens when a mortal attracts the attention of the gods, Psyche faced this fate because she had become the victim of jealousy. Resenting the attention Psyche received, Aphrodite had called upon her son Eros to exact her revenge.

Aphrodite: Eros, I want you to do something about this Psyche. In keeping with the directives of the oracle, her parents have dressed her for marriage and abandoned her on a mountaintop. Go there and make sure that she falls in love with the most horrible, despicable monster you can find.

Eros: Do you have someone in mind, Mother?

Aphrodite: No, son. I am just so weary of hearing about her beauty, and I want her out of my sight. Just do this for me in whatever fashion you wish.

Narrator 2: Eros descended to the mountain summit where he found Psyche, sleeping soundly. Just like mortals, he was struck by her beauty and took pity on her. He decided he couldn't give her to anyone repulsive but must have her for himself. He quickly devised a plan that would keep his treachery secret but would allow him to have her all to himself. With the help of Zephyrus, Psyche was transported to a magnificent palace. She woke in the darkness to his quiet voice.

Eros: Psyche, wake up. You have nothing to fear, my dear.

Psyche: Where am I?

Eros: Don't worry about that, you're safe. When daylight comes, you'll see that you are living in a beautiful, comfortable palace. You'll want for nothing.

Psyche: But who are you? Let me light the lamp so I can see you.

Eros: No, my dear. You need to trust me. Understand that I can only visit you at night and that you can't ever look upon my face. Will you agree?

Psyche: Are you so terrible that I can't look upon you without revulsion?

Eros: Of course not, Psyche, but it is better that you trust me.

Narrator 1: The young couple talked through the night, and Psyche gradually came to trust Eros's kind, loving manner. During the day, Psyche wandered the grounds of the palace, enjoying the pleasant rooms and lush gardens. Each night, her affection for Eros grew, and she was by and large content with her fate. Her days were long, however, and she became lonely. Finally she entreated Eros to let her see her sisters.

Psyche: Dear, I have a favor to ask of you.

Eros: You know I would grant almost anything to you, Psyche. Has something made you unhappy?

Psyche: The time I spend with you is wonderful, but my days are long. I miss my family and wondered if I could see my sisters.

Eros: I don't think that would be wise, Psyche. You know you can't leave the palace.

Psyche: I know, but what is to stop them from coming here for a visit? It needn't be long, and even a brief visit would sustain me for a long time. I do miss them so.

Eros: Well, I suppose if they came here it would be all right. But it can only be a short visit.

Psyche: Of course, dear. I promise that it will be just the briefest of visits.

Narrator 2: When her sisters arrived, Psyche's luxurious home and way of life impressed them.

Sister 1: Psyche, it appears that we were worried unnecessarily. This is a magnificent palace.

Psyche: Yes, it is lovely, isn't it? And my husband is really charming.

Sister 2: But I don't understand. It was foretold that you would be married to a monster. What is he like? How can the prophecy be so wrong?

Psyche: He's not a monster but is kind and loving. I couldn't be happier than when he is with me.

Sister 1: What do you mean by that? Doesn't he live with you?

Psyche: Of course he does.

Sister 2: Then let's meet him. We're so eager to meet him and see what he looks like.

Psyche: I'm afraid that's impossible.

Sister 1: I don't understand.

Psyche: I've never seen him.

Sister 2: Psyche, you're talking in riddles. You seem to be in love with him, but you've never seen him? This doesn't make sense.

Psyche: It's an unusual arrangement, I admit. You see, he only comes at night, and he won't allow me to light a lamp. So I've never really seen him.

Sister 1: Then he *must* be a monster as the oracle foretold.

Psyche: No! I don't believe he is. He has been nothing but loving and charming. I know in my heart that he's a wonderful man.

Sister 2: He is deceiving you, Psyche, and it's time you found out who he truly is.

Psyche: But he's forbidden me to look at him. Although I am curious, of course....

Sister 1: Forget that. You *must* look at him. Just light a lamp one night when he's asleep and take a quick peek. He'll never know, and you'll have your curiosity satisfied.

Psyche: I'll think about it, but let's talk of other things now.

Narrator 1: Their visit soon came to a close. That night, Psyche thought about all they had discussed and decided she couldn't resist one quick look at her beloved husband. She quickly lit her lamp and looked down at the sleeping form of a truly splendid young man. Psyche gasped with joy and leaned closer, spilling a drop of oil on his sleeping form.

Narrator 2: Eros woke up and faced her, shaking with anger.

Eros: How could you disobey me, Psyche? You've ruined everything! Why couldn't you believe in me? What happened to the love I showed you? Couldn't you trust me? Good-bye, Psyche, for this is the end for us.

Narrator 1: With those final words of reproach, both Eros and the palace disappeared, leaving Psyche bereft and frantic with despair.

Psyche: What have I done? Why did I listen to my sisters?

Narrator 2: Psyche began to wander the world, praying to the gods for help in finding her beloved. Aphrodite pursued her, putting her through a variety of terrible ordeals. Eros, watching from afar, became increasingly convinced that Psyche indeed loved him. After her journeys led her to a brief visit to the Underworld, Eros took pity on her and went to Zeus to ask him to intervene.

Narrator 1: Zeus agreed that Psyche had shown incredible devotion and strength of character. He declared that she would be immortal. He gave permission for Eros to marry Psyche, and all of Olympus celebrated their marriage. Even Aphrodite abandoned her jealousy and rejoiced with the gods and goddesses.

HELEN

Although many variations on the legend of Helen exist, this story focuses on her marriage to Menelaus, her elopement with Paris, and the war that followed between the Greeks and the Trojans. Helen relied on her beauty and typically is seen as a rather passive figure who let others control her. She knew that the gods controlled her fate, however, having given her the great beauty that incited passion and wars. The stories of her birth vary. According to the story featured in the following script, Zeus took the shape of a swan to court Leda. One of Leda's eggs held Helen, who grew to be a beautiful woman. Helen's parents struggled to find her an appropriate husband. Menelaus was chosen, but after their marriage, Helen and Paris fell in love and eloped to Troy. Menelaus followed, using the hollow horse to overcome his enemy and retrieve Helen. Helen's adventures continued after her famous rescue from the Trojans, and students may want to investigate versions other than the one presented here.

Presentation Suggestions

Place Helen in the center of the stage with Paris on one side and Menelaus on the other. Place them on stools so that they dominate the stage. Narrator 1, King Tyndareus, Leda, and Odysseus can stand on one side. Narrator 2, Hera, Athene, and Aphrodite can stand on the other side of the stage.

Props

The women should be dressed in flowing, rich clothing, appropriate for royalty and goddesses. King Tyndareus should be dressed in royal clothing. Paris and Menelaus should be dressed in battle clothing. Create a backdrop with a large wooden horse by a walled city.

Delivery Suggestions

Paris should sound quiet and somewhat passive. Menelaus should sound more forceful and aggressive. Helen has only a few lines and should sound sweet and compliant. Although their roles are brief, Hera, Athene, and Aphrodite should sound persuasive. All other speakers should use normal voices consistent with their roles.

Characters

- 回 Narrator 1
- 回 Narrator 2
- 回 King Tyndareus
- 回 Leda
- 回 Helen
- 回 Odysseus
- 回 Hera
- 回 Athene
- 回 Aphrodite
- 回 Paris
- 回 Menelaus

HELEN

Narrator 1: Zeus looked down from Olympus and saw that Leda was a beautiful woman, so he disguised himself as a swan and courted her. Some time later, Leda laid two blue eggs. One egg held Helen and her brother Pollux, offspring of Zeus and therefore immortal. The other egg held Clytemnestra and Castor, born of Leda and her mortal husband, King Tyndareus.

Narrator 2: Castor and Pollux, dedicated half brothers, grew up to be fine athletes. Castor tamed horses, and Pollux became a skilled boxer. Clytemnestra grew up to be a beautiful young woman, but no one was more beautiful than Helen. Soon King Tyndareus had to find husbands for the two women.

King Tyndareus: Leda, it's time that Clytemnestra and Helen found suitable husbands.

Leda: Agamemnon has expressed interest in Clytemnestra, and as King of Mycenae, he would make a fitting husband.

King Tyndareus: Let's proceed with plans for that marriage. But what about Helen? So many young men seek her favor.

Leda: Let's discuss this with her. Perhaps she has a favorite.

Narrator 1: Helen's parents asked her to meet with them to discuss her future.

King Tyndareus: Helen, it's time that you married. Do you have any favorites among your suitors?

Helen: No, Father. There are so many of them that I can't keep them straight.

Leda: So none have caught your fancy, dear?

Helen: No, Mother. Some are princes; some are handsome; some are kind. They all seem charming—and most persistent!

Leda: Will you be satisfied if we make the decision for you?

Helen: Of course, mother. I know you want the best for me.

Narrator 2: After Helen left, her parents continued to discuss how to resolve the problem of whom to choose as Helen's husband.

Leda: Odysseus would have made a fine husband, and he made some initial inquiries. But when he saw all the other suitors, he withdrew.

King Tyndareus: Why?

Leda: I'm not sure. Why don't you summon him and ask?

Narrator 1: King Tyndareus did as Leda suggested, and Odysseus joined them.

King Tyndareus: Greetings, Odysseus.

Odysseus: Your majesty . . . how may I be of service?

King Tyndareus: Leda tells me that previously you showed some interest in our fair Helen, yet you withdrew from the courting process. Why?

Odysseus: There are so many men who wish to marry her. I feared that if I succeeded, all others would fall to fighting about her. I have become quite fond of Penelope and will seek her hand.

King Tyndareus: You've shown that you are wise and that you care about our people. Do you have any ideas how we might forestall problems with the men who don't win her heart and hand?

Odysseus: Perhaps this strategy would work. Ask the suitors if they will stand by your choice. If they say yes, then ask if they'll promise to help should someone try to steal her.

Leda: Another wise idea, Odysseus. It's worth a try, don't you think, Tyndareus?

King Tyndareus: Yes, Leda. Let's inform Helen and then assemble everyone for the announcement.

Leda: I'm glad you've chosen a suitor for her, dear.

Narrator 2: Helen was summoned and appeared before her parents.

Helen: Have you made a decision, Father?

King Tyndareus: Yes, I've chosen Menelaus of Sparta. He'll make a fine husband, and you'll grace their kingdom. Could you be happy with Menelaus, Helen?

Helen: Yes, Father. I find him pleasing. But what about all the other suitors?

King Tyndareus: Don't worry about that, dear. We have a plan, thanks to Odysseus's wisdom. We've asked the suitors to swear their allegiance and stand by the final decision. They've agreed, and should someone try to thwart our plans, they will fight for your honor.

Narrator 1: Helen married Menelaus and lived happily with him. Years passed, and her fame as the most beautiful woman in the world spread far and wide. Meanwhile, the people of Sparta didn't realize that a young prince of Troy was about to become an instrument of change and war. Some years before, Priam and Hecuba received an omen that their youngest son, Paris, would one day destroy Troy. Instead of killing Paris, they abandoned him on Mount Ida, where shepherds raised him.

Narrator 2: Paris grew to be exceptionally handsome and skilled in games. Once, when he returned to Troy to participate in the games, his sister Cassandra recognized him. Zeus was particularly impressed with his beauty, and when the gods began squabbling over who was the most beautiful goddess, Zeus decided Paris should determine the winner.

Narrator 1: Zeus told Hermes to take Athene, Hera, and Aphrodite to see Paris and determine which should be designated the most beautiful. The winner would receive a golden apple. Each of the goddesses wanted to win and offered a reward to Paris in exchange for the golden apple.

Hera: Choose me, Paris. If you do, I shall give you all of Asia to rule. You would have great honor and even greater power.

Athene: Paris, don't listen to Hera. Choose me and you will be both wise and skilled in combat. You will be admired for your wisdom and will never lose in battle.

Aphrodite: Ah, Paris, I can offer you love. If you say I am the most beautiful, I will give you the love of Helen of Sparta.

Narrator 2: Aphrodite chose to ignore the fact that Helen was married, and Paris found her offer irresistible.

Paris: Aphrodite, you have truly found a way to sway me, for who wouldn't want to have the love of the most beautiful woman in the world? The golden apple is yours.

Narrator 1: Paris departed for Sparta, entering the palace where Helen and Menelaus held court. Eros shot his arrow of love in Helen's heart as she gazed on this splendid young man. Meanwhile, Menelaus departed to attend a funeral, giving Helen and Paris the opportunity to elope. Helen was so infatuated with Paris that she abandoned her home, leaving behind her young daughter Hermione.

Narrator 2: When Menelaus discovered Paris's treachery, he reminded Helen's former admirers of their promise to defend her honor. They assembled a huge fleet and set sale for Troy. The brave warriors set up camp outside the city, waiting for the battle to begin. But first, Paris agreed to discuss the dilemma with Menelaus, hoping to come to a peaceful resolution.

Paris: Menelaus, you are wasting your time if you think your fleet of ships can conquer us. Look at the high walls that surround us. You'll never get past them.

Menelaus: Paris, I don't want to risk the lives of my fellow warriors, but you knew I couldn't let you kidnap Helen.

Paris: But I didn't kidnap Helen. She willingly left with me.

Menelaus: That may be, but I know she still loves me, and we have a daughter to raise!

Paris: Well, you've come all this way, so you must have had a plan.

Menelaus: Let's be fair and settle it between us. If you truly love her, you should be willing to fight for her. And I don't mean for you to send out soldiers to fight on your behalf. This fight is between us—just the two of us—and the winner will have Helen.

Narrator 1: Paris was uneasy with this plan, but Menelaus left him little choice. He preferred leisurely pursuits to combat, but he agreed reluctantly to Menelaus's proposal.

Paris: All right, Menelaus. Let's arrange the combat.

Narrator 2: The duel began, and Menelaus had the advantage until Aphrodite sent a blanket of fog, making it impossible to see. Menelaus could not find Paris, and the battle went unresolved. Menelaus retreated to the camps, and a full-scale battle began, raging on for nearly a decade. During this time, the gods watched as the Greeks and Trojans fought, with some gods and goddesses taking sides. Finally Zeus ordered them to let the mortals decide their own fates.

Narrator 1: The Greeks were unable to penetrate the walls of Troy, but they had an equally impressive defense in Achilles. The son of Thetis, Achilles had been dipped in the river Styx, making him invulnerable except where Thetis held his heel when immersing him in the magic waters. Although Paris was not a particularly skilled marksman, Apollo guided him as he drew back his arrow. The arrow struck Achilles in the heel, mortally wounding this favorite hero.

Narrator 2: The Greeks took immediate revenge on Paris and killed him with a poisoned arrow that Heracles gave to Philoctetes. The Greeks then prepared to depart, seemingly giving up the battle. They boarded their ships, leaving behind a gift for the Trojans, a large wooden horse. The Trojans triumphantly drew the horse into the city, regarding it as a fine trophy of war.

Narrator 1: But in the dead of night, this hollow horse opened up, and armed Greek soldiers stole out, ready to destroy Troy and capture Helen. After the bloody battle, very few Trojans survived. Aphrodite guided her son Aeneas along with his father Anchises, his wife Creüsa, and son Ascanius to Mount Ida, where he founded another city. Menelaus, enchanted as always by Helen's beauty, forgave her and set sail for home. After eight years of travels, Helen finally returned to Sparta with Menelaus at her side.

Heracles's story is one of the longest and most complex of the myths. Hera despised Heracles because he was the son of Zeus and Princess Alcmene. She tried to kill the son as an infant, but Heracles used his incredible strength to kill the serpents Hera sent. However, Heracles's strength worked against him when he killed his tutor, Linus. This was just the first of many murders, most instigated by Hera's meddling. To atone for his misdeeds, Heracles had to complete ten labors or tasks. Heracles completed twelve labors over a period of many years, becoming increasingly famous for his heroism. Once released from his labors, he continued fighting in many campaigns. Finally, Heracles's beloved wife, Deianeira, was tricked into poisoning him, and Heracles ascended to Mount Olympus on a cloud. Because of the episodic nature of Heracles's lengthy story, this script is divided into three acts. The Muses assist Heracles and others in the description of his adventures.

Presentation Suggestions

Have the following characters sit on chairs in this order: Narrator, Polyhymnia, Clio, Calliope, and Erato. Have the following characters stand behind the other characters in this order: Melpomene, Terpsichore, Euterpe, Thalia, and Urania. The following characters should sit on stools to one side: Eurystheus and Heracles.

Props

The Muses can have props appropriate to their gifts: sheet music for Polyhymnia, a history book for Clio, poetry books for Calliope and Erato, a map of the stars for Urania, a tragedy drama mask for Melpomene, dance shoes for Terpsichore, a flute for Euterpe, and a comedy drama mask for Thalia.

Delivery Suggestions

The characters can use normal voices, but they should practice their parts to ensure a smooth delivery.

Characters

- ◙ Narrator
- ◙ Polyhymnia
- ◙ Clio
- ◙ Calliope
- ◙ Eurystheus
- ◙ Heracles
- ◙ Urania
- ◙ Erato
- ◙ Melpomene
- ◙ Terpsichore
- ◙ Euterpe
- ◙ Thalia

HERACLES

Act One: The First Four Labors

Narrator: The Muses loved to gather together and share their stories. In this story, they tell the tale of Heracles, also called Hercules. Descended from Danaüs, his mother was Princess Alcmene, granddaughter of Perseus and Andromeda. His father was Zeus, so Hera hated Heracles and his twin brother, Iphicles. When the twins were about eight months old, Hera sent two spotted serpents into their cradle. But even as a baby, Heracles was extremely strong. He simply grasped the serpents and squeezed them to death. But let's hear from the Muses, who have come to tell us other stories about Heracles.

Polyhymnia: Heracles enjoyed learning, but he didn't appreciate having to learn how to sing and play the lyre. Iphicles was a willing student, but Heracles was rebellious. One day their tutor, Linus, had to scold Heracles to get him to pay even the slightest attention. Linus became so annoyed that he raised his hand to strike Heracles. That was Linus's last act. Heracles picked up a stool and crashed it down on Linus's head. For this, Heracles was brought before the tribunal for judgment, but he quoted an ancient judgment of Rhadamanthys, which states that one can kill an aggressor in self-defense. Heracles was acquitted.

Narrator: That is when he was sent to the country, wasn't it?

Clio: Yes, he was in charge of Amphitryon's herds of cattle, but his education continued. Teutarus taught him archery, Castor taught him how to handle arms, and Eurytus taught him how to use a bow.

Polyhymnia: Don't forget that Eumolpus continued his musical education!

Clio: That's right. But by the time Heracles was eighteen years old, he knew he must atone for murdering Linus. He consulted the oracle of Delphi, who told him he'd have to perform ten labors for Eurystheus, the King of Mycenae. Eurystheus was a weak man, and Hera used his weakness to manipulate him into setting forth increasingly difficult challenges for Heracles.

Calliope: Hera hoped that someone—or something—would bring an end to Heracles. But she was soon to be surprised. Heracles had more strength and cunning than Hera ever could have imagined. Let's listen to what happened.

Eurystheus: Heracles, I've brought you here to do my bidding. As you know, a monstrous lion is stalking and killing many of Amphitryon and Thespius's herds. The lion has a hide so thick and tough that no arrows can pierce it. It lives in a cave with two exits, so no one can corner it.

Heracles: I've heard of this lion. It is actually one of Echidna's offspring, which Zeus had allowed to live as a challenge to future heroes, isn't it?

Eurystheus: That's right. I want you to kill that beast. Do you think you can do it?

Heracles: I will use all my powers to fulfill your request.

Clio: In spite of the beast's thick hide and its great size, Heracles was up to the task. He blocked the cave's exit, drove the lion back into its cage and then used his incredible strength to squeeze the lion to death. After using the lion's own claws to skin it, he delivered the skin to Eurystheus, and his first labor was completed.

Urania: Remember that Zeus honored Heracles's skill by adding the lion to the constellations.

Narrator: That's right, he did. But that's just the beginning of his labors.

Erato: I'll pick up the story from here. A lot happened before Heracles's second labor. On his way home from killing the lion, he met messengers from Erginus, the king of Orchomenus. Each year they collected tributes from the Thebans. Heracles decided it was time for this practice to stop. He cut off each man's nose and ears and hung them on a rope around his neck. Then he told the messengers to take back the noses and ears as their tribute! Erginus was furious and immediately marched against Thebes. But Heracles defeated them and avenged himself further by requiring them to pay a tribute that was double the amount that had been requested!

Narrator: And this is when Creon, the king of Thebes, rewarded Heracles by giving him his eldest daughter, Megara, in marriage.

Melpomene: That's right, and Iphicles married her sister. Megara had several children with Heracles, and this should have been a happy time for him. But Heracles never learned to control his rage. There have been many rumors as to exactly what happened, but all we know for sure is this: Heracles killed his children. Some say he threw them into the fire. Others say he killed them with his bow and arrows. If it hadn't been for Athena's intervention, he even would have killed his own father. Athena saw what was happening and struck Heracles, rendering him unconscious.

Narrator: But why would he kill his children?

Melpomene: That has never been clear, but many think Hera was responsible for Heracles's acts of madness. Also, he was simply so strong that he could kill with ease. Some say that Hera hoped he would do something so despicable, he'd be forced into exile. Anyway, Heracles became so worried about Megara's safety that he gave her to his nephew Iolaus.

Narrator: Let's hear about the Hydra, who was involved in his second labor.

Eurystheus: Heracles, you were clever with the lion. Let's see if you can perform this task. You've heard of the Hydra who is the offspring of Echidna and Typhon, haven't you?

Heracles: Yes, it is a snake with many heads that breathe out poisonous air.

Eurystheus: That's right. It kills anything that it comes near, from crops to people. Conquering that Hydra is your next challenge.

Erato: Heracles took his nephew Iolaus along and asked him to keep a fire burning in the forest while he held his breath and began his attack. Heracles used every weapon he had, including arrows and a saber, to attack the Hydra. He'd destroy one head, and a new one would grow up in its place. Finally, he began having his nephew give him burning brands so he could cauterize the stumps of the heads.

Narrator: But wasn't the main head immortal?

Erato: The story has it that the central head was indeed immortal, but Heracles cut it off, buried it, and put a huge rock on top of it. Then he rendered his arrows poisonous by dipping them in the Hydra's blood. Hera was so angry at Heracles's success that she sent a huge crab to help the Hydra. But the crab only managed to nip Heracles in the heel before Heracles crushed it. Heracles returned to Eurystheus.

Heracles: Eurystheus, I've destroyed the Hydra, as you requested.

Eurystheus: So I've heard. Don't think you can rest, young man. This time you won't be able to simply kill a creature. Instead you must capture it.

Heracles: What shall I capture?

Eurystheus: A dreadful boar with fearful tusks lives on Mount Erymanthus. You must bring it back alive!

Terpischore: Heracles began chasing the boar all over the mountain, yelling at it relentlessly. Finally, he chased the boar into the snow, where it sank to the tops of it massive legs. Heracles caught it and then dragged and rolled it down to the gates of Mycenae. Eurystheus was so terrified when he saw the beast that he hid himself in an urn! Finally, he came out to give Heracles his fourth labor.

Eurystheus: There are five hinds, all larger than bulls, with gilded horns.

Heracles: Those are the ones Hera captured, aren't they?

Eurystheus: That's right. She wanted four to pull her chariot. She let the fifth one roam freely, wearing a collar with an inscription that it was dedicated to Artemis. I want you to kill that hind.

Heracles: How can I do that? Killing a sacred beast is an impious act.

Eurystheus: Forget about impiety. Kill the beast.

Euterpe: So Heracles chased the hind for a year. It finally became tired enough that Heracles could wound the animal as it tried to cross the river Ladon in Arcadia. Then Heracles caught it and began to carry it on his shoulders. As he was passing through Arcadia, he met Artemis and Apollo, who accused him of wanting to kill a sacred animal. After a brief exchange, Heracles convinced them that he was only carrying out Eurystheus's directive, so he was allowed to continue on his way, completing his fourth labor.

Act II: The Next Four Labors

Narrator: For his first four labors, Heracles killed a lion, destroyed the Hydra, captured the boar, and killed the hind. Upon his return, he faced another daunting challenge.

Eurystheus: You've done well, Heracles, but do you think you can outwit the Stymphalian birds?

Heracles: I know little of them, except that they live in the forest on the shores of Lake Stymphalus.

Eurystheus: Like the hind, they ruin the crops in their relentless quest for food. No one can destroy them because their feathers are made of brass. One brass feather striking the head of a mortal causes certain death.

Heracles: I've heard rumors that the birds then make a meal of their victims.

Eurystheus: I've heard that's true. Another complication is that the forests are nearly impenetrable.

Heracles: Don't worry, Eurystheus. I have some ideas. *(To the audience)* I'll use the skin of the lion I killed in my first labor for protection. I'll create a din by striking together bronze castanets. I'll use poison arrows to kill the birds as they fly out of the thickets to escape the noise.

Thalia: As he planned, Heracles killed many of the birds. The few that escaped never returned.

Narrator: This completed Heracles's fifth labor. His next task was particularly distasteful.

Eurystheus: Heracles your next challenge involves King Augias, the son of Helios, the Sun. Augias has huge herds of cattle, but he never cleans his stables. Piles of manure lay everywhere. Not only is the entire area unsightly and repulsive, the manure is damaging the soil in the region. Your task is to clean the stables. Don't think it will be easy, Heracles. It's a huge task.

Urania: But Heracles was not only capable of the challenge, he also issued his own challenge to King Augias. Heracles bragged that he could clean the stables in a day. When King Augias scoffed, they entered into a bet. If Heracles succeeded, part of the kingdom would be his.

Narrator: What happened?

Urania: Heracles wasted no time in diverting the course of two rivers through the stable yards, washing the manure across the land. Heracles returned to Eurystheus's throne.

Heracles: I've completed the task of taking care of the manure.

Eurystheus: That may be, but you made a mistake, Heracles.

Heracles: There was no mistake. I completed the task, as you directed.

Eurystheus: But you placed a wager with King Augias, and you won. You've been compensated with part of his kingdom. Therefore, the completion of this task does not bring you any closer to being finished with your labors.

Narrator: Seems as if Eurystheus was determined to make Heracles's life miserable.

Polyhymnia: He had no choice. Hera was pressuring him to assign increasingly difficult labors. Wait until you hear about the seventh labor!

Eurystheus: Perhaps this time you'll limit yourself to the task at hand, Heracles. I know you've heard about how Minos promised to sacrifice anything that appeared in the sea to Poseidon. He fulfilled that promise until he saw how beautiful the Cretan Bull was.

Heracles: I heard that Minos was so struck by its beauty that he sacrificed a different bull.

Eurystheus: That's right. Of course, this infuriated Poseidon, who got his revenge by making the Cretan Bull untamable. For your next labor, bring the bull to me—alive.

Polyhymnia: Heracles tried to get Minos to help him, but Minos told him he would have to do it alone. Eventually, Heracles caught the bull, and according to witnesses, he rode on its back as it swam to Greece. After presenting the animal to Hera, Eurystheus wanted to dedicate it to her, but she freed the bull instead. It eventually wandered to Attica.

Narrator: Heracles returned to Eurystheus for his eighth labor.

Eurystheus: I am sure you know King Diomedes, ruler of Thrace. He owns four mares that eat any stranger who ventures onto his land. Bring back the four mares—alive.

Clio: Heracles traveled to Thrace, taking along some volunteers. After subduing the grooms in charge of the horses, they began to lead the mares away. But when they reached the beach, the local citizens attacked them. As Heracles fought back, the mares killed his companion, Abderus, who was a son of Hermes. Heracles killed the local inhabitants and then killed Diomedes, the king. He fed Diomedes to the mares, taming the horses in the process. After returning with the mares, he presented them to Eurystheus and was ready to accept his next assignment.

Act III: The Final Four Labors

Narrator: After killing many of the Stymphalian birds, cleaning King Augias's stables, capturing the Cretan bull, and capturing four mares, Heracles was ready for his next labor. Eurystheus's daughter, Admete, gave Heracles his ninth labor. Can you tell us about it, Calliope?

Calliope: Admete sent Heracles to the Amazons' kingdom to capture Hippolyta's girdle. The girdle had once belonged to Ares who had given it to Hippolyta as a symbol of his power over her. Once again, Heracles took some volunteers with him as he sailed to Themiscyra, the port of the Amazon's land. Hippolyta was ready to give him the girdle, but Hera intervened. She disguised herself as an Amazon and spread a rumor that Heracles was going to abduct their queen. Soon they were engaged in a battle. While common Amazons fought in the battle, the noblest challenged Heracles directly, fighting him individually. But Heracles won battle after battle. After Heracles captured their great leader, Melanippe, Hippolyta traded the girdle for Melanippe's freedom. Heracles believed that Hippolyta had betrayed him, and a battle followed. In the course of the fighting, Heracles killed Hippolyta.

Narrator: Didn't Heracles have another adventure on his way home?

Calliope: Yes. He was off the coast of Troy when he found Laomedon's daughter, Hesione, chained to a rock. Laomedon had promised Poseidon a reward for building the walls of Troy, but Laomedon betrayed Poseidon. In retaliation, Poseidon sent a sea monster to destroy Troy. Laomedon, desperate to stop the sea monster, offered his daughter as a sacrifice to save his land. When he saw Heracles sailing by, he begged Heracles to help him. Laomedon promised to give Heracles some splendid horses that had been a gift from Zeus to his father. Heracles waited for the monster, and when it rose out of the water with its mouth wide open, Heracles dived into it and cut its entrails to ribbons. He emerged without a scratch. But once again, Laomedon broke his word, and Heracles left without the promised horses.

Narrator: If Eurystheus had accepted all of Heracles's efforts, this would be his last labor, but things didn't go smoothly for Heracles, even though he continually succeeded in his tasks. He returned to Eurystheus.

Eurystheus: For your next labor, you must journey to the island of Erythia, far to the west in the gulf of Gaderia. Geryon, the great giant who lives there, owns a fine herd of cattle that is guarded by another giant, Eurytion.

Heracles: I've heard of Geryon. He is huge, with three bodies, three heads, six arms, and six feet. No mortal has ever dreamed of challenging Geryon. I'll need help, Eurystheus.

Eurystheus: Do what you must, but kill the monster.

Narrator: What did he do first?

Erato: Heracles knew he would need help, so first he organized his armies on Crete. Then they sailed to his first landing at Libya. He had various adventures there, killing the giant Antaeus and all beasts of prey. Finally, he came to a valley where two rivers met. There he founded the city of the hundred gates. Heracles found the heat of the Libyan Desert intolerable and decided to use his arrows to shoot down the sun. The sun begged him not to shoot, and Heracles suggested a trade. Each day, Helios crossed the ocean in a huge vessel, the *Cup of the Sun.* Heracles knew that if he had this vessel he'd be able to reach Erythia easily. When threatened by Heracles's arrows, the sun had no choice but to agree to the arrangement. Melpomene, why don't you continue with the story?

Melpomene: Well, Heracles still had obstacles ahead. He reached Iberia where the three sons of Chrysaor camped with their vast armies. Heracles challenged their leaders to combat and killed them without even involving the armies. He went on to Erythia and was met with Geryon's two-headed dog. Heracles raised his club and killed the dog with one blow. Then he killed Eurytion, who was guarding the cattle. Heracles started off with the cattle, but Geryon followed and engaged him in a grim battle. Hera appeared and tried to help Geryon. But Heracles shot an arrow into her breast, and she fled. Heracles prepared his bow again, carefully aiming an arrow at the exact place where Geryon's three stomachs joined. Heracles hit the mark, and Geryon thundered to the ground, dead from his wound.

Narrator: How did Heracles get all those cattle back home?

Melpomene: He took the northern route, passing the coasts of Spain, Gaul, Italy, and Sicily. In Liguria, he fought off an army of natives, running out of arrows in the course of the battle. The country had no stones, so Heracles asked Zeus for help. Zeus obliged by sending stones down from the heavens like rain. In Calabria, one of his bulls escaped and swam to Sicily, so Heracles simply swam after it. Hera tried again to stop him, sending gadflies, which attacked the herd and drove them mad. The herd scattered throughout the foothills of the mountains of Thrace. Heracles rounded up most of them, but some escaped and became the wild Scythian herds that wandered the hills. Finally he delivered the rest of the herd to Eurystheus, who sacrificed them to Hera.

Narrator: His eleventh labor was especially dangerous. Eurystheus had become desperate to best Heracles.

Eurystheus: Heracles, I want you to bring me Cerberus, the watchdog for the Underworld.

Heracles: Do you mean the dog with three heads, whose jaws drip venomous slobber?

Eurystheus: Yes, but that's not all. His body ends in a dragon's tail, and instead of hair, he is covered with snakes. You'll have to learn the secrets of the Underworld to complete this task, Heracles.

Terpischore: Zeus, recognizing the danger of this labor, asked Hermes and Athena to help Heracles. Heracles first had to be purified and then taught the secrets that would prepare him for the terrors he would face.

Narrator: How did Heracles get to the Underworld?

Terpsichore: Hermes escorted him there, where all but two of the dead, the Gorgon Medusa and the hero Meleager, fled when they saw him. Heracles drew his sword, but Hermes reminded him that the dead were empty shadows. Heracles met Theseus and Pirithous who were both still alive but were chained by Pluto because they had tried to rescue Persephone. Heracles was allowed to free Theseus, but Pirithous had to stay and continue his punishment. Heracles also released Ascalaphus, who was being held under a huge rock.

Narrator: Did Heracles ever meet with Pluto?

Terpischore: Yes, he finally reached Pluto and asked his permission to take Cerberus away. Pluto said he could, but only if he overpowered the dog without using the weapons he had brought with him, wearing only his breastplate and lion skin. Heracles agreed, and set out after Cerberus, who was crouching at the mouth of the Acheron. Ignoring the dog's thunderous barks from all three heads, Heracles grasped the dog's neck with his hands. He ignored the stings from the dog's forked tongue at the end of his tail and held on until the dog was overpowered. Heracles then returned to Earth, but once Cerberus saw daylight, he grew mad with fear and spewed venom all over the Earth. This caused the poisonous aconite plant to spring from the ground.

Narrator: Eurystheus was terrified when he saw Cerberus! Once again, Eurystheus hid in an urn. He didn't know what to do with the beast.

Eurystheus: Heracles, take that horrid animal back to Pluto! Then you can complete your final labor.

Heracles: What will I do, Eurystheus?

Eurystheus: Long ago, when Hera married Zeus, Gaia gave her golden apples as a wedding present. Hera planted them in a garden near Mount Atlas, but the daughters of Atlas would steal the apples. To protect her precious fruit, Hera had a dragon with one hundred heads guard the tree. Find the tree and bring me three apples.

Heracles: But how am I to find the garden?

Eurystheus: That is for you to figure out.

Narrator: How did Heracles find the garden?

Euterpe: The only person who knew where to find the tree was Nereus, the Old Gray Man of the Sea, and he refused to tell Heracles. When Heracles seized Nereus to squeeze the secret out of him, Nereus began changing shapes, taking on the form of all kinds of animals. But Heracles held on until Nereus told him that the garden was west of the setting sun, close to where the Titan Atlas stood, holding up the sky. Heracles set out toward the setting sun. He had many adventures on the way. When he climbed the Caucasus, he found Prometheus being tortured by an eagle that ate away his liver every day. Prometheus told Heracles that he'd never be able to collect the golden apples. Only a god could pick the apples of immortality. Then Prometheus said the only way Heracles could get them was to have Atlas pick the three golden apples for him.

Narrator: How did Heracles convince Atlas to help?

Euterpe: Atlas was quite naturally weary from holding up the sky, so Heracles offered to hold the sky while Atlas collected the three golden apples. Atlas agreed, but after getting the apples, Atlas told Heracles that he himself was taking the golden apples to Eurystheus while Heracles continued to hold up the sky. Heracles agreed, but asked Atlas to hold the heavens while Heracles put a cushion on his shoulders. As soon as Atlas had resumed his burden, Heracles picked up the apples and fled, eventually delivering the apples to Eurystheus.

Narrator: That was his twelfth labor. Was Heracles finally free of these challenges?

Thalia: Zeus was very pleased with his son, for Heracles had become the most famous hero on Earth. Heracles traveled all over Greece, helping many people with more heroic deeds. This infuriated Hera, so she made him insane for a time. While mad, Heracles killed many men, angering Zeus. This time Zeus determined Heracles's punishment, sentencing him to serve for three years as a slave to Queen Omphale of Lydia. She made him wear women's clothes and sit at her feet sewing and spinning. After three years of such humiliation, Heracles was humbled.

Narrator: What happened after he was released from his punishment?

Urania: Heracles became a great soldier, leading many successful campaigns. He married Deianeira, the love of his life, after winning her in a fight with the river god Achelous. They had a son and enjoyed their life together. But Deianeira's intense love for Heracles led to his death. During a journey together, the centaur Nessus tried to steal Deianeira. Heracles shot an arrow into Nessus's heart, mortally wounding him. As Nessus lay dying, he convinced Deianeira that a potion made of his blood would ensure that Heracles would always love her. Sometime later she decided to use it, dipping Heracles's tunic in it. When he donned the cloak, the poison was activated, and Heracles knew he was dying. Deianeira could not bear this, and in her grief, she committed suicide.

Narrator: Heracles ended his life with great dignity. He ordered his servants to build him a funeral pyre and to light the fire. They all refused, except for Philoctetes, who lit the fire. Heracles rewarded Philoctetes by giving him his bow and arrows. The sky opened with a clap of thunder, and Heracles ascended to Mount Olympus on a cloud, leaving us only stories of our beloved hero.

HERMES

Also known as Mercury (in Latin), Hermes means "pillar," relating to the symbol of the cairn or pile of pebbles described in this script. Hermes's mother, Maia, was the daughter of Atlas, and his father was Zeus. Hermes is known for many roles: the god of crossroads, of commerce, of thieves, and of travelers. He is also known as a trickster and is pictured as having winged feet. In this story, shortly after being born, Hermes steals Apollo's sheep, creates a lyre and flute, and becomes Zeus's trusted messenger. His role as the escort to the Underworld is mentioned briefly. Hermes has minor roles in many myths, making related stories ideal for a series of scripts.

Presentation Suggestions

The characters should stand in the following order: Narrator 1, Maia, Zeus, Hermes, Apollo, Hera, and Narrator 2.

Props

Hermes could have golden wings attached to his feet. In addition, wings could be added to a helmet. Maia should be dressed simply, with Hera dressed in more regal clothing. A set of Panpipes and a lyre could decorate the stage. Consider using flute music to introduce and conclude the script.

Delivery Suggestions

Hermes should sound clever and convincing as he defends his behavior. Maia should support and defend her son. Apollo should change his delivery to reflect his anger and later his desire to own the lyre and flute. Zeus should sound amused and proud of his son. Hera should be angry when she speaks to the council.

Characters

- ◙ Narrator 1
- ◙ Maia
- ◙ Zeus
- ◙ Narrator 2
- ◙ Hermes
- ◙ Apollo
- ◙ Hera

HERMES

Narrator 1: Zeus had many wives, which made Hera extremely jealous. Zeus managed to keep secret one wife, Maia, who was the daughter of Atlas and Pleione, which made Maia one of the Pleiades. She lived in Arcadia on Mount Cyllene in a cave so deep that Hera never discovered she was one of Zeus's wives. On one of Zeus's visits, Maia greeted him with news of the birth of his son.

Maia: Zeus, meet Hermes, your son.

Zeus: He looks like he will grow to be an adventurous young man and a fine son, Maia.

Narrator 2: Hermes was more than adventurous; he was especially mischievous. He grew quickly, leaving behind the basket in which his mother had placed him, and toddling to the pasture where Apollo kept a large herd of cattle.

Hermes: Look at these fine cows! What does Apollo need of so many? I could use some for myself, and if I am clever, I think I can steal them without anyone knowing. Let me think. . . . I know, I'll tie these branches to their tails so their footprints will be brushed away. Just to ensure their escape, I'll make them walk backward. Apollo will never know what happened to them!

Narrator 1: Hermes got the cows ready and forced them to walk backward out of the pasture. He even disguised his own footprints so it appeared as if a giant had taken them away. Soon he got back to Mount Cyllene, where he killed and sacrificed two of the cows to the gods.

Narrator 2: But Hermes wasn't finished yet. Keeping the entrails of the sacrificed cows with him, he hid the other cows and returned to his cave. He found a tortoise outside his cave.

Hermes: Why, what is this tortoise doing here? I think I have a use for it.

Narrator 1: Hermes killed the tortoise and cleaned it out. Then he stretched the cows' entrails across the hollow shell, creating the first lyre. He slipped back into his basket and pretended to be asleep. But Maia knew he had been out making mischief.

Maia: Where have you been, Hermes? Have you gotten yourself into trouble?

Hermes: Of course not, mother, but I have done something that will help both of us. But for now, just listen to this music.

Narrator 2: Hermes played on the lyre until his mother fell asleep. Meanwhile an oracle had told Apollo what had happened to his herd, and Apollo hurried to Maia's cave.

Apollo: Maia, are you aware of what your son has been doing? He's a thief of the worst kind!

Maia: How can you say that? Look, Apollo, he's sound asleep in his basket.

Apollo: I suspect he hasn't been there long! Hermes, wake up! I know you've stolen my cows, and I want them back now!

Hermes: How could I steal your cows? I'm practically a baby and haven't ever seen a cow in my young life. Do you see any cows in here? Look around for yourself if you don't believe me.

Apollo: You are a thief *and* a liar, Hermes! Let's go to Olympus and settle this!

Narrator 1: Apollo chased Hermes up to Olympus, where the gods were quite amused at the sight of a powerful god chasing a youngster to Zeus's feet.

Apollo: This youngster is not only a thief, but also a liar! He stole my cows and claims innocence. Tell him to give back my cows at once!

Zeus: What do you have to say for yourself, Hermes?

Hermes: Father, how could I steal his cows? I've only been alive a short while. There certainly aren't any cows in my mother's cave.

Zeus: Perhaps there are no cows in the cave, but I suspect you know where they are. I think it's time to resolve this, Hermes. Take Apollo to the cows, son.

Hermes: All right, Father, I'll take Apollo to them.

Narrator 2: Hermes took Apollo to the herd of cows, but when Apollo realized that two were missing, he asked Hermes what had happened to them.

Hermes: I confess. I used two of them as sacrifices to the gods, but I also made this wonderful instrument.

Narrator 1: Hermes began to play the lyre, and his playing enchanted Apollo.

Apollo: Hermes, would you trade some cows for the instrument? It makes exquisite music.

Hermes: I want to keep the lyre, Apollo, so just take your cows and return them to the pasture.

Apollo: You don't understand, Hermes. I'm the god of music and must have that lyre!

Hermes: How many cows will you give me?

Apollo: I'll give you the entire herd!

Hermes: Give me the herd and your magic wand.

Apollo: All right, Hermes, the cows and magic wand are yours.

Narrator 2: Hermes looked after his fine herd carefully, but one day he became bored and cast about for something to amuse him. He picked up a reed and began to blow on it like a whistle. Then he began to experiment with different lengths of reed and soon was making music with the flute he had created. Once again, Apollo had to add this instrument to his collection.

Apollo: Hermes, I have heard you playing a new instrument. I want to have it.

Hermes: What will you give me for it, Apollo?

Apollo: I'll give you the golden crook I used when I was caring for my herd.

Hermes: I'll take that, but I also want you to teach me the art of soothsaying.

Apollo: Once again, you drive a hard bargain, but I'll agree and teach you a few other useful skills as well.

Narrator 1: Apollo and Hermes became devoted friends as Apollo taught Hermes how to tell fortunes using pebbles. Hermes became known as a trickster because he enjoyed pranks, many of them harmless. But one act wasn't a prank. Some time ago, Zeus had fallen in love with the mortal Io. Hera was about to catch them, and Zeus changed Io into a cow. Realizing what he did, Hera charged Argus, her hundred-eyed servant, with guarding Io. Zeus had asked Hermes to figure out a way to free Io, and Hermes had told a never-ending story that put Argus to sleep Then he killed the servant. Hera demanded that Hermes be punished.

Hera: I have brought the council together to judge Hermes. I am giving each of you a pebble to cast your vote. As you know, Hermes killed my servant Argus. If you find him guilty, cast your pebbles at my feet. If you find him innocent, cast your pebbles at Hermes's feet. But to be fair, Hermes, let me ask if you have any words of defense?

Hermes: It's true that I went to Argus, but I only offered to tell him a story to pass the time. After all, he had become understandably bored while watching that cow. Now tell me, is it a crime to bore someone to death?

Narrator 2: The gods applauded Hermes's defense and cast their pebbles at Hermes, burying him in the process. In fact, if you see piles of stones along the road, you'll know that the spirit of Hermes still stands inside, showing you the way.

Narrator 1: Zeus became increasingly impressed with Hermes and requested his presence.

Zeus: Hermes, you have proven to be an intelligent and ambitious young man. I am going to give you a special role, but you must continue to use your gifts well.

Hermes: Of course, Father.

Zeus: I am going to put wings on your feet to take you over the sea and Earth with speed and ease. You can be my messenger, but you must keep my trust.

Hermes: Thank you, Father. I'll try not to disappoint you.

Narrator 2: Hermes served his father and other gods in many ways. One of his more somber tasks involved escorting souls to and from the Underworld. But he often performed heroic deeds, killing the Giant Hippolytus, saving Ares and Zeus, assisting travelers, and protecting shepherds. Travelers around the world recognize his winged feet and helmet as he performs his tasks as divine messenger.

JASON AND THE GOLDEN FLEECE

As a child, Jason was sent to Chiron, a centaur, to be raised and trained in the heroic skills and arts. His father, Aeson, had lost the throne to his brother, Pelias, and Aeson feared that Pelias would harm Jason. Jason grew to be a handsome, powerful young man, and when Aeson died, Jason returned to his home to take the throne from his uncle. Hera, who helped Jason with the many quests he had to carry out to reclaim the throne, befriended him. His primary goal, to find and retrieve the golden fleece, involved a variety of famous heroes, such as Heracles, Meleager, and Theseus. As they sailed through the seas, they visited many islands, barely escaping capture or defeat on many occasions. Finally, Medea helped Jason as he captured the golden fleece. But Medea's jealousy and vengefulness led them to a tragic end.

Presentation Suggestions

This script has many characters. Arrange them using chairs and stools or have the minor characters leave the stage after their speaking parts. Place the three narrators on one side of the stage, sitting on chairs. On the other side of the stage, place Hera, King Pelias, Hypsipyle, and Nurse on chairs. Jason and Medea can sit on stools in the center of the stage. Heracles, King Aeëtes, King Phineus, and Circe can stand in the center in front or on either side of Jason and Medea.

Props

Use a nautical theme, with a large backdrop or mural of a ship. The heroes should be dressed in traveling clothes, such as short tunics. The stage can be decorated with swords and shields. King Pelias can wear royal clothing. Hypsiple and Nurse can wear gowns. Medea can wear black, in keeping with her tragic role.

Delivery Suggestions

The narrators should carefully rehearse their lines and be familiar with the background they provide. Jason should sound confident and royal. King Pelias should sound crafty. Medea should sound supportive, desperate, and vengeful in turn. In general, the other characters should use normal voices.

Characters

- ◉ Narrator 1
- ◉ Narrator 2
- ◉ Jason
- ◉ Hera
- ◉ Narrator 3
- ◉ King Pelias
- ◉ Hypsipyle
- ◉ Nurse
- ◉ Heracles
- ◉ King Phineus
- ◉ King Aeëtes
- ◉ Medea
- ◉ Circe

JASON AND THE GOLDEN FLEECE

Narrator 1: Cretheus had founded the kingdom of Iolcus on a bay of Thessaly, creating a great city. He had two sons, Aeson and Pelias, and he gave the throne to Aeson, his older son. Pelias, a jealous and power-hungry man, usurped the throne. Aeson feared for his son Jason's life, so he sent Jason to the centaur Chiron to be raised and trained in the skills befitting a royal heir and hero. Soon after, Aeson died, but Jason became strong and even more handsome than he was as a child.

Narrator 2: After twenty years with Chiron, Jason decided to return to Iolcus to reclaim his father's throne. He made a striking sight as he walked along. His golden hair hung to his shoulders, and he wrapped his powerful body in a panther skin. He carried two spears, one for throwing and one for thrusting. As he approached a river, he saw an old woman and stopped to offer her his help.

Jason: Do you need to cross the river, ma'am?

Hera: Why yes, young man. I would be grateful for any assistance you can offer.

Jason: If you don't mind sitting on my shoulder, I'll carry you to the other side.

Hera: You're a kind young man.

Narrator 3: Jason didn't realize that this was Hera, disguised as an old woman. He started to wade across, but with each step she grew heavier. When he was halfway across, his feet began to sink deep into the mud. He lost one of his sandals, but he continued steadfastly until he reached the other shore.

Hera: You are indeed a fine mortal. Now I must tell you who I really am. I am Hera, and I shall reward you for your exceptionally kind nature. I know that you hope to regain the throne from Pelias, and I will support your efforts.

Jason: Your patronage will be most welcome. I have no knowledge of the challenges that I face, but knowing you are on my side gives me strength.

Narrator 1: King Pelias had grown much older by this time. For many years, he had puzzled over an oracle's prophecy that one day a youth with only one sandal would bring danger. When Jason arrived in Iolcus, the people gathered around him, curious to know who this golden-haired youngster was. King Pelias came down from his throne to see the stranger and paled when he saw that the young man wore only one sandal. He questioned the youth about how he came to be in Iolcus.

King Pelias: Good morning, young man. Welcome to Iolcus. Where do you come from, and what brings you to our city?

Jason: I was the son of King Aeson, but Chiron has raised me. I've come to visit my father's house.

King Pelias: Welcome! Let me show you the palace. We'll have a feast to celebrate your return!

Narrator 2: King Pelias sounded welcoming and pleasant, but in truth, he was alarmed at Jason's arrival. And as the uneasy king expected, by the sixth day, Jason was ready to make his claim.

Jason: King Pelias, I appreciate the kindness you have shown me, but I know that everything you possess is truly mine. But I'll be fair and let you keep the herds of cattle and sheep and the fields on which they graze—even though you took them from my parents. All I ask of you is the scepter and the throne that was once my father's.

King Pelias: Jason, you're a fine young man, and I know you want to rule in your father's stead. To be an effective leader of the kingdom, however, you must prove that you are heroic. It's true that I am aging, and the people need a leader they can admire. Not only do you need to show that you can be a strong leader, but you also need to win over the people you'll be ruling.

Jason: I'm sure you have something in mind. What do you propose?

King Pelias: Before I tell you the task, you must hear a story. Athamas, the king of Boeotia, had a son named Phrixus. Ino, Phrixus's stepmother, mistreated him and wanted to kill him. Wanting to save him, his own mother, Nephele, set Phrixus and his sister, Helle, on the back of a winged ram, whose fleece was pure gold. They rode over land and sea on the magical ram.

Jason: I heard that Helle was lost during their journey.

King Pelias: Yes, the flight made her dizzy, and she fell to her death in the sea, thereafter called the Sea of Helle. But Phrixus held on and was delivered safely to King Aeëtes in the land of Colchis, on the coast of the Black Sea. He was received warmly and married one of King Aeëtes's daughters. In gratitude for his safe journey, Phrixus sacrificed the ram to Zeus and presented the golden fleece to King Aeëtes. In turn, King Aeëtes offered it to the god Ares and nailed it to a tree in a sacred grove.

Jason: I've heard that many people have tried to get the fleece from that grove.

King Pelias: That's true, Jason. But an oracle had told King Aeëtes that his life depended on keeping the golden fleece in his possession. So he consigned a dragon that never sleeps to guard it. I want that fleece. Complete this quest, and you'll have the kingdom and scepter.

Jason: Give me timber and men to build a sturdy ship. Once I have the ship and worthy men at my side, I'll begin the quest.

King Pelias: You'll have what you need.

Narrator 3: Jason didn't realize that King Pelias hoped Jason would lose his life in the process. He gave his word to the King that he would return with the treasure. Jason summoned Argus, the best shipbuilder in Greece, to build a light, seaworthy ship. Then Jason asked for volunteers among the heroes of the day. The crew included the most exalted heroes of the Argonauts: Heracles, Lynceus, Admetus, Meleager, Menoetius, Theseus, Euphemus, and others. As they set sail, Orpheus inspired them with his music, and Poseidon sent the West Wind to fill their sails as they headed east.

Narrator 1: The heroes rowed together with high spirits. Gradually, however, they grew tired until the only ones left rowing were Jason and Heracles. Never wanting to back down from a challenge, each continued to row to see who would be deemed the strongest. Just as Jason fainted from exhaustion, Heracles's oar broke in two, and the unspoken competition ended in a draw.

Narrator 2: The Argonauts landed on the island of Lemnos, inhabited by women who had killed their husbands out of jealousy a year before. The women feared they would be attacked by the Argonauts. So when they saw the ship approaching, they prepared for a battle. When Jason and the others saw the contingent of women warriors, they sent a herald, requesting shelter and time to rest. Hypsipyle, the queen, and her nurse discussed their options with the other women.

Hypsipyle: Sisters, we have killed men out of jealousy, and now these men seem to seek our favor. We don't want them to find out what we did, but perhaps we should send them provisions and let them be on their way. What do you think, Nurse?

Nurse: Send the provisions, but think about what might happen should the Thracians ever come. These men could defend us. We've only been without men for a year, but who is going to tend the fields and draw the ploughs? And someday you will want to have children. I'm old and won't be here many more years, but you younger people need to think about your futures. I advise you to trust these strangers and ask them to stay and govern your city.

Narrator 3: The women agreed with her proposal and sent words of welcome to the heroes. Jason and many others entered the city, eager to meet the many beautiful women. Heracles and a few others stayed behind, preferring to remain on the ship. When Jason came to meet with Hypsipyle, she flattered him with her attentions.

Hypsipyle: Jason, you are welcome in our city. We have no men here to fight you, and we value your patronage. If you find favor with this country, we would like you to stay. In fact, I would be honored if you would take the scepter and rule over the people.

Narrator 1: Of course, Hypsipyle omitted the fact that the women had killed their husbands out of jealousy.

Jason: Our people are grateful for your help, but you must keep your scepter and your island. I have a journey ahead and must complete a task I've promised to do.

Hypsipyle: I appreciate your dedication to your undertaking, but I hope you'll accept our gifts and hospitality in the meantime.

Jason: We will all welcome a respite from our traveling, fair queen.

Narrator 2: Indeed, the women of Lemnos provided the heroes with lavish gifts and feasts. They stayed an extra day, and then another, and then another. The men found it increasingly difficult to leave the beautiful island with these accommodating women. Finally Heracles left the ship and came to the island, where he chastised them.

Heracles: Men, think about what you are doing! You have families at home. Do you really want to stay here and tend the fields for the women of Lemnos? If Jason wants to stay and marry Hypsipyle, he can do that. But let's return to our homes instead of languishing on this distant island.

Narrator 3: The men, including Jason, knew that Heracles spoke wisely and prepared to go. The women were disappointed, and Hypsipyle bade farewell to Jason.

Hypsipyle: Jason, may the gods lead you to the golden fleece so that you can fulfill your quest. But should you ever wish to return, my scepter awaits you. I know that you won't return, but I hope you'll at least think of me.

Jason: Hypsipyle, you'll always be in my heart, but I must fulfill my destiny. Good-bye.

Narrator 1: The heroes pulled at their oars, and the island of Lemnos soon disappeared from sight. Winds swept the ship toward the island of Cyzicus where savage giants with six arms lived next to the peace-loving Doliones, descendants of the sea god. The Doliones's king greeted the heroes and treated them hospitably. The Argonauts anchored their ship, and all but Heracles went ashore. While Jason told the king of his quest, the men climbed the island to determine the location of the island.

Narrator 2: Meanwhile, giants were laying down a wall with huge stones so they could close off the harbor. Heracles saw them at their mischief and shot many of them with his arrows. The other heroes finished off the rest of the giants when they returned. Planning to follow the advice offered by the king, they sailed out to sea. But the night wind blew them back to Cyzicus. The peace-loving Doliones thought they were being attacked, not recognizing Jason and the heroes in the dark. A fierce battle ensued, and Jason killed the king who had so recently befriended him. The Doliones fled to their city, and it wasn't until morning that everyone realized their dreadful mistake. The heroes stayed for three days, sharing in the grief over the tragedy.

Narrator 3: The heroes next landed in the bay of Bithynia where the Mysians greeted them with kind hospitality and a fine feast. Heracles, never one to engage in the comforts offered at such events, went into the woods to find a pine tree for a new oar. His beloved friend Hylas was filling his jar with water when a nymph in the pool captured him, pulling him to the bottom of the pool. When Heracles discovered what had happened, he threw down the pine tree and bellowed with grief as he ran off.

Narrator 1: The heroes meanwhile prepared to depart, and when the wind came up, they left without Heracles. After more adventures they came upon the land where King Phineus suffered greatly. The harpies would not allow him to eat, and he had become quite frail. According to an oracle, the Argonauts would save him. He greeted them weakly, but with great hope.

King Phineus: You are welcome here. An oracle foretold that you would help me. Can you stop the harpies?

Jason: Let us try, King Phineus.

Narrator 2: Two of the heroes pursued the harpies, but they couldn't quite catch them. Then suddenly, Iris, messenger of Zeus, appeared and told them that the harpies would no longer trouble King Phineus. The heroes prepared a celebratory feast. King Phineus addressed the heroes.

King Phineus: I am grateful for what you have done. Here is what you must do now. Travel to the Symplegades in the narrows of the Euxine Sea. These rocky islands float in the water and the current drives them together and then apart.

Jason: I've heard of these islands. Ships rarely pass between them without being crushed by the islands coming together.

King Phineus: Here are your directions. Take a dove with you and release it as you near the island. Pass through the islands quickly, following the dove's straight flight. Only then can you avoid being destroyed. Next, you'll sail past many rivers, coasts, the Amazons, and the land of the Chalybes, who dig iron out of the Earth. Finally, you'll come to the Coast of the Colchis, where the river Phasis pours into the sea. You'll see the palace of King Aeëtes where a sleepless dragon guards the gold fleece hanging at the top of an oak tree.

Jason: Thank you, King Phineus. With your help, we may succeed and be able to return to our homes before long.

Narrator 3: The heroes followed the dove, barely making it between the islands. After a dangerous journey, they reached their destination. They knew that King Aeëtes had a reputation for killing foreigners. While Jason and a few companions approached King Aeëtes's palace, the rest of the heroes stayed aboard the ship. Soon Jason was explaining their quest to King Aeëtes.

Jason: Greetings, King Aeëtes. I am Jason and I have come with a ship full of heroes to retrieve the golden fleece. If you give us the fleece, all of Greece will honor you. Of course we are ready to repay you for any help you offer. If there is a war we can fight or a wrong we can right, just name it.

King Aeëtes: If you are indeed great heroes, you'll find the labor I request of you to be trivial. I have two fire-breathing bulls that graze in the field of Ares. I plow the field with them, and then sow the field with the teeth of a dragon. The crop I harvest is men, whom I slay with my lance. If you can accomplish this in a day, as I usually do, you may take the golden fleece.

Jason: That is indeed a challenge, but we will try.

King Aeëtes: There is more, Jason. If you do not succeed, I shall cut out your tongues and lop off your hands. That will be the end of your heroic deeds!

Narrator 1: Of course, King Aeëtes did not know that Hera was helping Jason. She had sent Eros to shoot his arrow into Medea, King Aeëtes's daughter. Medea fell instantly in love with Jason. That night she sent for him and offered her help.

Medea: Jason, I called you here because I want to help you.

Jason: How can you help, Medea?

Medea: I have been trained in the art of magic and have prepared a magic salve for you.

Jason: How will that help?

Medea: Neither fire nor iron can harm he who covers himself with the salve.

Jason: Why would you give me this? Your father is surely hoping we will fail. I can't believe that he truly wants to give us the golden fleece.

Medea: Jason, can't you see in my eyes how I feel about you? I would do anything to help you. Now listen as I tell you what to do. After my father gives you the dragon's teeth for sowing, bathe alone in the river waters. Put on black garments and dig a pit. Prepare a fire, slaughter a lamb, and sacrifice it on the fire. Offer honey from your own cup to Hecate and then leave. Do not look back for any reason.

Jason: What about the salve?

Medea: The next morning, cover yourself with the ointment. You'll be protected and feel very strong. Cover your lance, sword, and shield. When the men spring up from the dragon's seed, throw a stone among the men. They will fight over it and you can kill them. The magic only lasts one day, but that should suffice.

Jason: Medea, if this works, I will remember you every day for the rest of my life. Tell me, Medea, how can I repay you?

Medea: There is a way, Jason. I yearn to live in Greece instead of this dreadful kingdom.

Jason: If I succeed, I swear I'll make you my queen and take you away from here.

Narrator 2: With Medea's help, Jason carried out the task exactly as required. But King Aeëtes had no intention of giving him the golden fleece. While King Aeëtes plotted to kill the Argonauts, Medea sneaked to the ship and called for Jason.

Jason: Medea, what are you doing here?

Medea: Jason, my father will never let you have the golden fleece. Even as I speak, he plots his attack on your ship. You must leave immediately.

Jason: But we'll never get the golden fleece if we go now.

Medea: But you can. Take me with you, swearing that you will do right by me when I am an alien in your land. I can show you where the golden fleece is and put the dragon to sleep for you.

Jason: Medea, I swear by Zeus and Hera, that you will be my honored wife once we have returned to Greece. Let's be off then.

Narrator 3: Medea guided the ship to the sacred grove and sang the dragon to sleep with a sweet-voiced prayer. Jason pulled the fleece down while Medea sprinkled the dragon's head with a magic potion. Jason carried the fleece above his head, and it shimmered like a beacon as they returned to the ship. When they boarded the ship, he spoke to his fellow heroes.

Jason: As you can see, we have the golden fleece. We would not have succeeded if it hadn't been for Medea's intervention and guidance. In return I shall take her as my wife. She has saved us all, along with all of Greece. Soon King Aeëtes will discover what we've done and pursue us. Here's my plan: Half of us should take up the oars and make haste with our retreat. The other half should hold up our shields for protection.

Narrator 1: Without delay, they began rowing away as quickly as possible. Meanwhile, King Aeëtes had learned that the ship had departed, and he mounted a fleet of ships to pursue them. He desperately wanted his revenge on Jason for stealing his daughter. King Aeëtes's ships were lighter and faster, and they lay in wait for Jason's ship at the mouth of the Ister River. The two sides decided to negotiate, agreeing that Jason could take the golden fleece, but Medea would stay behind on another island. A nearby king would serve as an arbitrator and determine if Medea should be returned to her father. Medea was furious at Jason's betrayal.

Medea: Jason, what are you thinking of? How can you betray me? What about your promises, your solemn oath? I gave up everything for you and betrayed my father. Don't leave me here alone. You know that if I'm returned to my father, his punishment will be harsh.

Jason: You're right, Medea. This negotiation was just a ploy to delay the battle until we can determine what to do. Everyone who lives here would help your brother capture you so he could take you back to your father. He is a strong leader, the one we must defeat.

Medea: There's no going back for me, Jason. You should know that by now. Here's an idea: Carry forward as if you were going to honor the negotiation. We'll hold a banquet, get my brother alone, and kill him. They will have to end their pursuit to bury him.

Narrator 2: As Medea and Jason carried out the murder, Zeus looked on with anger. Nothing was worse than killing a family member. The sacred and magical oak, which was among the timbers of the ship, told the heroes that until Circe purified them of the murder, they would wander the seas. Indeed, the winds and waves tormented the ship until they found Circe's palace.

Narrator 3: Medea knew how Circe, her father's sister, would change men into animals and convinced Jason to let her accompany him to Circe's palace. Circe greeted them quietly, having heard about their crimes.

Circe: Hello, my niece. What brings you here?

Medea: Circe, I know I have committed grievous acts, but it was only out of love. Jason was searching for the golden fleece for honorable reasons. I only wanted to help him succeed. I had not anticipated falling in love with him.

Circe: You have committed a grave wrong, but you have given up your homeland as well. Your father will never forgive you.

Medea: I know, Circe, but we still need your help before we can continue to Greece. What's done is done. Won't you take pity on us and help?

Circe: Yes, Medea. I don't condone what you have done, but I will make a sacrifice to Zeus on your behalf. But you must leave. I want no more of this tragic affair.

Narrator 1: Jason and Medea returned to the ship, gentle winds sent them on their way back to Greece. They still had many challenges. The Sirens, half birds and half women, would sing so beautifully that sailors who heard them would abandon their ship and dive into the waters toward them. To evade their power, Orpheus sang and played his lyre, drowning out their songs.

Narrator 2: The ship also had to pass through a narrow strait guarded by two monsters. Scylla looked like a woman above the waist, but six snarling dogs grew out of her hips. Charybdis greedily sucked passing ships into her huge gullet. But the daughters of Nereus helped the heroes. At Hera's bidding, they swam around the ship, guiding it past the monsters and around the rocks.

Narrator 3: After more challenges, the ship finally returned to Greece, but King Pelias was still determined to keep Jason from his goal. Again Medea intervened, tricking King Pelias's daughters into killing him. But the people were so horrified at Medea's series of crimes that the throne went to Acustus, Pelias's son, instead of Jason.

Narrator 1: Jason left for Corinth and married Medea, as promised. They had three sons, and Jason loved her for ten years. Then he fell in love with Glauce, the daughter of Creon, king of Corinth. When he told Medea that he wanted a divorce, she was furious. When the wedding to Glauce proceeded, Medea sent a magic robe to Jason's bride, killing her and setting the entire palace on fire.

Narrator 2: When Jason rushed to Medea to avenge his bride's death, he found that Medea had killed their children to punish him. He searched frantically for Medea, discovering that she was disappearing into a dark cloud in a carriage drawn by two dragons.

Narrator 3: In a final act of despair, Jason pulled out his sword and thrust it into his heart, joining his sons forever.

KING MIDAS

According to legend, ants collected grains of wheat and marched them up to King Midas's mouth when he was an infant. This indicated that he would be wealthy. Indeed, the story of King Midas's choice to turn everything he touched into gold is so well known that "the Midas touch" is a familiar phrase. Less familiar is King Midas's poor judgment when asked to help determine whether Marsyas or Apollo was the finer musician. After Midas chose Marsyas, Apollo punished Midas by giving him the ears of an ass. (In this version, the word donkey has been substituted for ass.) Although Silenus is identified as the son of Pan in this story, some versions describe Silenus as having been born from drops of Uranus's blood when Cronus mutilated him. Silenus is also described as being the son of Hermes and a nymph.

Presentation Suggestions

Place the narrators on one side of the stage. Consider having King Midas sit on a chair, raised on a platform to indicate his royal status. The other characters can stand on either side of King Midas. If preferred, Marsyas, Apollo, and the barber can enter for the second portion of the script.

Props

The stage can be decorated to have a royal setting. Consider placing as many gold-colored objects on stage as possible. Panpipes and a lyre can be placed on stage or held by Marsyas and Apollo. The barber should be dressed simply, while the other characters can have robes or fine clothing.

Delivery Suggestions

King Midas should sound greedy when he makes his wish and turns objects into gold. Although not considered intelligent, he was sincere in ruling his kingdom. The reader should have him sound grieved at the loss of his daughter. Marsyas should sound vain. Apollo should sound powerful and vengeful. The barber should sound obedient and simple.

Characters

- ◙ Narrator 1
- ◙ King Midas
- ◙ Silenus
- ◙ Narrator 2
- ◙ Dionysus
- ◙ Daughter
- ◙ Marsyas
- ◙ Apollo
- ◙ Barber

KING MIDAS

Narrator 1: King Midas, the ruler of Phrygia, was known for his kindness. One day, some peasants came across a stranger sleeping after having too much wine. The peasants didn't recognize their hostage as Silenus, son of Pan. Dionysus had raised Silenus, learning to love wine a bit too much. The peasants woke him and brought him in chains to King Midas, who recognized him.

King Midas: Silenus, I apologize for any mistreatment you have suffered at the hands of my subjects. I fear they didn't recognize you. Let me bring you food and drink. Please make yourself comfortable, Silenus, and I will be your humble servant. These foolish peasants will be punished for their mistakes.

Silenus: Thank you, King Midas. I am truly grateful that you have treated me with respect. But do not punish your peasants. They thought they were helping to protect your people. I admit that I was sleeping in a rather unusual place. And after a long night of revels, I must have looked quite unsavory.

King Midas: That may indeed be true, but let's get you refreshed with food and a bath. My servants will bring you clean garments.

Silenus: Thank you, King Midas. I appreciate your attentive kindnesses.

Narrator 2: When Silenus was feeling himself again, he and King Midas engaged in several enjoyable conversations. Silenus was a wise man, and King Midas, though not especially intelligent, was an eager conversationalist. Finally, it was time for Silenus to depart.

Silenus: King Midas, you have been a generous host. I would like to repay you.

King Midas: No, Silenus. No repayment is necessary. It is I who is in your debt for sharing my home and giving me such good company.

Silenus: Nevertheless, I am going to ask Dionysus to grant you a gift. And now, I am off to my home.

Narrator 1: True to his promise, Silenus asked Dionysus to bestow a favor on King Midas. Dionysus went to see King Midas.

Dionysus: King Midas, you showed great kindness to Silenus, and I am going to grant you a wish. You may have any wish you desire, but I urge you to choose wisely.

King Midas: I don't have to think about this wish, Dionysus. I would like for everything I touch to turn into gold.

Dionysus: Then your wish is granted.

King Midas: Thank you! This is quite grand! I'll be the richest man on Earth!

Narrator 2: King Midas ran through his home, touching every object and marveling at the cold beauty of the glittering room.

King Midas: A gold chair! A gold table! Gold dishes to eat on! Bring me food! I want to eat on these fine dishes!

Narrator 1: But when King Midas tried to eat, all the food turned to gold.

King Midas: What is this? How can I eat? I must figure out a way to eat or I'll die.

Narrator 2: Just then, King Midas's daughter came running into the room, now glittering from all the gold objects.

Daughter: Father, what has happened? Why is everything so beautiful?

King Midas: Dionysus granted me a wish, my dear. Everything I touch turns to gold.

Daughter: Father, can you turn my doll into gold?

King Midas: Yes, my love, but think carefully before you ask me to do that. Perhaps it won't be as much fun to play with when it is hard and heavy.

Daughter: But it will be beautiful! And priceless!

King Midas: Nothing is as beautiful and priceless as you, my daughter.

Daughter: Thank you, Father!

Narrator 1: Then, before King Midas could utter another word, his beloved daughter ran forward and threw her arms around her father.

King Midas: Noooo!

Narrator 2: King Midas wept golden tears as he held the daughter that was the most precious belonging in the world to him. Her golden curls hung stiff, and her face was frozen in a loving smile. King Midas fell to the ground in grief.

King Midas: Dionysus, if you can hear me, I beg you to reconsider this favor. My wish has turned into a curse. Please, please—return my daughter to me. All the gold in the world is not as precious as my daughter!

Narrator 1: Dionysus took pity on King Midas and appeared before him.

Dionysus: I warned you about choosing wisely. Here's what you must do. Go to the spring at the source of the river Pactolus. Wash your head and hands in the spring. This will undo the curse.

Narrator 2: King Midas followed Dionysus' directives and soon held his living daughter in his arms again.

Narrator 1: Some time later, King Midas showed poor judgment again. In a previous time, Perseus had cut off the head of Medusa, the terrible Gorgon who could turn men to stone with one look. Knowing how dangerous the head could be, Perseus had given it to Athena, who had fastened it to her breastplate.

Narrator 2: Athena had taken two of Medusa's bones and made them into a double flute. When Athena played, she puffed out her cheeks, amusing all who looked at her. One day she saw her image in her shield and realized why others were laughing at her. She threw down the flute, cursing it.

Narrator 1: Marsyas, a satyr, found it and began playing it. He played the flute beautifully, but he fell victim to his pride.

Marsyas: Listen to me play this glorious flute! I can play two tunes at once. Not even Apollo can do that!

Narrator 2: Apollo was listening and wasted no time in confronting Marsyas.

Apollo: So, Marsyas, you claim to be a finer musician than I?

Marsyas: Listen, Apollo! You can't play like this!

Narrator 2: And Marsyas played a delightful duet on his double flute.

Apollo: That may be clever, but no one bests me!

Marsyas: There's only one way to resolve this difference of opinion. Let's have a contest.

Apollo: Agreed! But if I win, your loss will be greater. You shall lose your hide.

Marsyas: I'm not worried. But who will judge our contest?

Apollo: The nine muses—who else holds the knowledge for such a competition?

Marsyas: And I choose King Midas as the final judge.

Narrator 1: The contest began. Apollo played his lyre with great skill, and then Marsyas played his flutes. The nine muses judged Apollo as the better musician, but King Midas disagreed.

King Midas: I vote for Marsyas. After all, he has mastered the art of playing two instruments at once.

Apollo: Ah, but can you do this?

Narrator 2: Apollo turned his lyre upside down and continued playing his lovely song. Marsyas turned his flutes upside down and began to blow. No matter how hard he tried, he couldn't make the flutes work.

King Midas: You have proven yourself, Apollo. You win the contest.

Apollo: And now, you both will pay for your folly.

Narrator 1: Apollo pulled the skin off Marsyas and made it into a drum. Then it was King Midas's turn for his retribution.

Apollo: King Midas, you are not a wicked man, just a stupid one. Your ears can't even hear when music is good. For that, you deserve ears as stupid as you are. From now on, you shall have the ears of a donkey.

Narrator 2: Suddenly, tall ears sprouted out of King Midas's head. He rushed to get a tall hat to cover them. From that moment on, King Midas always wore a tall, peaked cap, starting a new fashion among Phrygians. Before long, he had to go to his barber.

King Midas: You have been loyal to me for many years, and I trust you'll continue to honor me. I am about to remove my hat, but before I do, you must swear that you won't betray my trust by revealing what you are about to see. If you do, you'll face certain death.

Barber: Of course, your majesty. I would never betray you.

Narrator 1: The barber was stunned when he saw the ears, but he kept quiet as he groomed the king. This arrangement continued for many years. But finally the barber couldn't resist saying the secret out loud.

Barber: This secret has become a torment. I know what I'll do. I'll say it out loud in a safe place, just to hear the words. No one will hear, but I'll have it out of my system.

Narrator 2: The barber dug a hole in the ground and whispered into it.

Barber: King Midas has donkey's ears!

Narrator 1: The barber filled up the hole, thinking the secret was safe. But the nearby reeds had heard him, and as they swayed in the wind, they passed the secret along. Soon it spread all over the world.

Narrator 2: King Midas was so disgraced that he left his throne and went into hiding. After an illustrious rise to power, King Midas was reduced to living in the woods, hiding his ears and himself from the world.

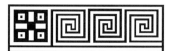

LETO

Leto, one of Zeus's many wives, was soon to give birth to twins. Hera, always jealous of Zeus's other wives, decreed that Leto could not give birth on any of the lands on Earth. When Poseidon gave her refuge on a floating, barren island, Hera decreed that the sun could not shine on Leto. Again Poseidon helped her, but Hera stopped Ilithyia, the goddess of childbirth, from attending Leto. Finally, Hera gave in to Iris, who offered Hera a necklace in exchange for letting Ilithyia go to Leto's aid. When Apollo and Artemis were born, Zeus rejoiced and gave them each a bow and a quiver of special arrows. Leto fled to Asia Minor to escape Hera's jealousy.

Presentation Suggestions

Place Narrator 1 on one side of the stage and Narrator 2 on the other side. Hera, Ilithyia, and Iris can stand next to Narrator 1. Leto should stand in the middle. Poseidon and Zeus should stand next to Narrator 2.

Props

The stage could have a mural behind it depicting a barren island with a lone palm tree on it, with waves arching above it. Hera and Zeus can be dressed in regal clothing. Leto can be dressed in more simple clothing. Iris could wear a necklace that she offers to Hera. Two bows and quivers of arrows could decorate the stage.

Delivery Suggestions

Hera should sound angry and jealous. Leto should sound desperate and discouraged. Poseidon should sound kindly and concerned. Ilithyia and Iris should sound pleading. Zeus should sound proud and happy about the birth of the twins.

Characters

- ◎ Narrator 1
- ◎ Hera
- ◎ Narrator 2
- ◎ Leto
- ◎ Poseidon
- ◎ Ilithyia
- ◎ Iris
- ◎ Zeus

LETO

Narrator 1: Leto, daughter of Coeüs and Phoebe, embarked on a long and dangerous journey. This was not a journey of choice, however; she traveled only to find a place where she could give birth to her twins. As one of Zeus's many wives, she was a target of Hera's jealousy.

Hera: Twins! How dare Leto bring twins into this world! I will fix it so that she'll never give birth to those children. I hereby decree that all lands refuse shelter to her!

Narrator 2: Leto wandered from Attica to all the islands of the Aegean Sea, but the people feared Hera's reprisals should they let her enter. Leto appealed to Poseidon, god of the sea, to help her.

Leto: Poseidon, do you have any hope for me? I need shelter so that I can give birth to my children. Hera has decreed that no one give me refuge.

Poseidon: I think I can help. I've raised a new island from the sea. It still floats freely, so it is not yet a true land. No people live there, and it only has a single palm tree on it, but you are welcome to stay there as long as you need. It's called Ortygia.

Leto: Thank you, Poseidon. I'll never forget your kindness.

Narrator 1: Leto made her way to Ortygia, anticipating her birth with joy.

Leto: At last I have found a place to give birth away from Hera's control. I have little time left to wait. After the birthing, I can decide what to do next.

Narrator 1: But Hera heard about Leto's arrival on Ortygia.

Hera: Leto thinks she has outwitted me, but I'm not done yet! I hereby decree that Leto can only give birth where the sun's rays never touch the ground!

Narrator 2: Leto heard of Hera's decree and appealed once again to Poseidon.

Leto: Poseidon, have you heard what Hera has done now? She says that I cannot give birth where the sun touches the ground. What shall I do?

Poseidon: Don't forget that I rule the seas, Leto. Watch my powers at work.

Narrator 1: With those words, Poseidon commanded the seas to rise and make a dome over the island. Darkness descended, and Leto gratefully awaited the day of the birthing. But Hera was not finished.

Hera: That pair of deceitful deities won't outwit me! Ilithyia, come to me!

Narrator 2: Ilithyia, the goddess of childbirth, heard Hera's command and rushed to see her.

Ilithyia: Hera, why do you call so urgently? How can I serve you?

Hera: Ilithyia, Leto is soon to give birth. I forbid you to go to her aid when her time comes.

Ilithyia: But Hera, Leto and the children will surely die!

Hera: That doesn't concern you, Ilithyia. Just do as I command.

Ilithyia: As you wish, Hera.

Narrator 1: Soon Leto began to have the pains of childbirth, calling out for Ilithyia's help.

Leto: Ilithyia, come to me! The pains are more than any goddess should endure.

Narrator 2: Ilithyia heeded Hera's stern decree and kept away, but all the other goddesses were moved by Leto's agony. After nine days and nine nights of pain, Iris devised a plan to convince Hera to relent. She flew to her, bringing a long a beautiful necklace, nine yards long, made of gold and amber.

Iris: Hera, I have a proposal for you, and hope you will consider it carefully.

Hera: What could you possibly offer me, Iris?

Iris: I have this necklace that I will give you in trade if only you will let Ilithyia go to Leto's side. Will you accept this offer?

Narrator 1: Hera couldn't resist the unusually beautiful necklace and agreed.

Iris: Thank you, Hera, for showing such compassion for Leto's suffering.

Narrator 2: Ilithyia flew to Leto's side, and soon Leto gave birth to a boy and a girl. The goddesses rejoiced to see a happy end to her suffering. Leto joyfully named her children.

Leto: My children shall be known as Apollo and Artemis.

Narrator 1: Poseidon rolled back the waves and gave the island a new name.

Poseidon: This island, now brilliant in the sun, shall forevermore be called Delos!

Narrator 2: Zeus was thrilled when he saw his new children and called them to him.

Zeus: My children, I have a gift for each of you, but you must use the gifts with care. Artemis, you are quick and nimble, and you shall be the goddess of the hunt and all newborn creatures. Your gift is this silver bow and a quiver full of arrows. Your arrows are soft as moonlight and will bring death, but the death will be free of pain. Apollo, I am also giving you a bow and arrows, but yours are hard and piercing. You will be the god of music, light, and reason. Do not abuse the trust I have placed in you.

Narrator 1: Zeus honored Delos for giving refuge to Leto and blessed the island. He fastened it to the bottom of the sea, and the island became lush and fertile, the richest of all the Greek Islands.

Narrator 2: Perhaps you wonder what happened to Leto. She knew that Hera would always hate her and fled to Asia Minor, where she could live in safety. Apollo and Artemis had many adventures, told in other tales.

MELAMPUS

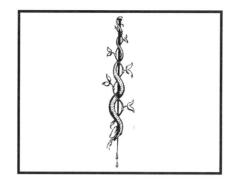

Melampus was a kind child who learned how to understand the language of animals after showing kindness to some motherless snakes. He tried to help his brother Bias steal a herd of cows but was caught and imprisoned. When Melampus heard worms discussing how the beams above him were about to collapse, he predicted that the roof would fall and insisted he be moved to another cell. The story of his prophecy led to other adventures in which he cured the offspring of two kings and gained riches in return. In this myth, Melampus's brother not only marries Pero, but also is granted King Proteus's daughter in marriage. Melampus marries King Proteus's other daughter and has five children with her.

Presentation Suggestions

Have the following characters stand in the back row in this order: Narrator 1, Idomene, Bias, Neleus, and Narrator 2. Have the following characters sit in chairs in the front: King Phylacus, Melampus, and King Proteus. Have the two vultures sit on the floor to one side of the stage.

Props

The setting can have an outdoor theme, with animals portrayed on a mural. The characters can wear clothing appropriate to their roles: The kings can wear royal clothing, and the other people can wear modest dress. The vultures can be dressed in black.

Delivery Suggestions

Normal voices can be used throughout the script.

Characters

- ◙ Narrator 1
- ◙ Narrator 2
- ◙ Melampus
- ◙ Idomene
- ◙ Bias
- ◙ Neleus
- ◙ King Phylacus
- ◙ Vulture 1
- ◙ Vulture 2
- ◙ King Proteus

MELAMPUS

Narrator 1: Melampus was the son of Amphythaon and Idomene. When he was born, his mother put him in the shade but left his feet in the sun. His feet were tanned by the sun, giving him his name, "the man with the black feet." He was a kind child who loved animals.

Narrator 2: One day Melampus was out walking with his mother when they happened upon a dead snake.

Melampus: Mother, look! This snake has died, leaving all these baby snakes alone.

Idomene: I wonder how she died, Son. Perhaps another animal crushed her.

Melampus: What will the babies do?

Idomene: They will probably die or be eaten by a hawk or other bird of prey.

Melampus: Mother, could I give the snake a proper funeral?

Idomene: Of course, son. That would be very thoughtful of you. Even the lowliest animals deserve respect when they pass out of this world.

Melampus: Mother, could I also make sure the babies survive?

Idomene: Yes, Melampus. Just remember that eventually they'll have to return to the wild.

Melampus: I know, but at least they'll be big enough by then to be safe.

Narrator 1: Melampus prepared a funeral pyre for the mother snake. He tenderly raised the babies. They were so grateful to him that they licked his ears with their tongues. This act purified his ears, and Melampus was able to understand the language of the birds and animals. He learned many secrets and became very wise. He learned about herbs as well and became quite skilled at healing the sick.

Narrator 2: But Melampus didn't always show good judgment. He left Thessaly with his brother Bias to visit their uncle Neleus in Messenia. Bias wanted to marry Neleus's daughter, Pero, and asked for permission during their visit.

Bias: Uncle, I am in love with Pero and want to make her my wife.

Neleus: You're a fine young man, Bias, but what do you have as a wedding gift?

Bias: Uncle, you know I have little in my own name.

Neleus: Then you have some work to do. Here is my proposal. I covet King Phylacus's herds of cows, and if you bring them to me I will grant you my daughter's hand in marriage.

Bias: But how am I to get them? They are in Thessaly!

Neleus: That's your problem, Bias. When you've solved it, come see me about the marriage.

Narrator 1: Knowing that Melampus was skilled with animals, Bias asked him for advice.

Bias: Melampus, I want to marry Pero, but Neleus insists I must bring him King Phylacus's herds as a wedding gift. Do you have any ideas about how I could accomplish this?

Melampus: What animal guards the herds?

Bias: I've heard stories about a fierce dog.

Melampus: Let's go there. I think I know how to accomplish this, although I fear I'll pay a dear price for helping you.

Narrator 2: Melampus used his skill with animals to steal the herds for his brother, but in the process, he was caught and imprisoned by King Phylacus. After almost a year in his cell, Melampus heard worms talking. They were in the beams of the roof and had eaten through the wood. They expected the roof to collapse shortly.

Narrator 1: Melampus insisted that he be transferred to another cell. At first his guard laughed at him, but Melampus was so insistent that the guard gave in. As soon as he was moved, the roof caved in. King Phylacus heard about Melampus's prophecy and asked to see him.

King Phylacus: Melampus, I hear that you have amazing powers.

Melampus: I have had some success, King Phylacus.

King Phylacus: Well, I have a proposal for you. I know you and Bias want my herd of cows, and I will give you a chance to obtain them.

Melampus: What do you need?

King Phylacus: My son has been sick since he was little. No one knows what is wrong with him. If you can cure him, the cows are yours.

Narrator 2: Melampus set to work. He slaughtered an ox and left the meat on the ground. Two vultures swooped down, filled their bellies, and then began to talk.

Vulture 1: What a fine feast that was!

Vulture 2: I haven't been this full since the feast of King Phylacus.

Vulture 1: I remember that feast! King Phylacus had sacrificed a ram to the gods.

Vulture 2: And his son was so little! When he saw his father with a bloody knife in his hand, the prince screamed and screamed.

Vulture 1: That's right! King Phylacus threw the knife in the nearby tree, wounding the tree nymph. She cast a spell on the boy, and he's been sick ever since.

Vulture 2: Too bad the king doesn't know that the knife is still in the tree. He could use it to break the spell.

Narrator 1: Melampus immediately went to the tree. He felt the bark until he noticed a slight bulge. He carefully dug out the blade and soaked it in some water. Then he took the rusty brew to King Phylacus.

Melampus: King Phylacus, I believe I can cure your son. Have him drink this brew I've prepared. He should be strong and healthy again very quickly.

Narrator 2: The rusty brew worked, and Melampus received the herd of cows as promised. He gave them to Bias, who then was allowed to marry Pero. Word of Melampus's great healing powers spread across the Earth. Many kings sought him out for help in curing their sick.

Narrator 1: One of the kings who requested his help was King Proteus. He had three daughters who had angered Hera when they treated a wooden statue of her casually. Hera had stricken them with leprosy. They were so crazed that they dashed around half-dressed, mooing like cows. King Proteus begged Melampus to help him.

King Proteus: Melampus, I'm sure you've heard about my daughters. Each one thinks she is a cow! I can't control them, and they are getting worse by the day. Can you help them?

Melampus: I can help, but it will cost you one-third of your kingdom.

King Proteus: That's outrageous! I can't afford to give you so much. I'll just have to find another way.

Narrator 2: Melampus left, but after only a short time, King Proteus sent for him again. This time Melampus brought his brother Bias along.

King Proteus: Melampus, I beseech you once again. Can you help me with my daughters? They are wandering all over the kingdom. It is an embarrassment beyond words.

Melampus: I'll help you, but now it will cost you more than one-third of your kingdom.

King Proteus: What do you want? Anything!

Melampus: It will cost you two-thirds of your kingdom!

King Proteus: I have no choice. Just cure them!

Narrator 1: Melampus hired some runners and sent them after the girls. They managed to herd them to Melampus, who forced them to drink a beverage prepared with special herbs. Although one died of exhaustion, the other two were healed.

Narrator 2: As promised, King Proteus gave Melampus and Bias two-thirds of his kingdom. He also gave a daughter in marriage to each of them as reward for saving them. Melampus and Bias lived long happy lives thereafter.

OEDIPUS

The story of Oedipus describes the tragic—and beautiful—story of a man determined to escape his fate. When the oracle tells King Laïus and his wife Jocasta that their son will kill his father and marry his mother, the horrified parents abandon their baby. The child, eventually called Oedipus, is rescued and raised lovingly by King Polybus. Later, Oedipus learns of the prophecy from the oracle. Assuming that he would kill his beloved adoptive parents, he flees. During a confrontation along the way, he indeed kills King Laïus, not realizing that his victim is actually his father. He then marries Jocasta, with whom he has several children. Many years pass before Oedipus discovers the truth. In great sorrow, Jocasta kills herself, and Oedipus blinds himself. The gods realize that Oedipus committed these unspeakable acts unwittingly, but Oedipus cannot be consoled. He wanders the Earth, accompanied by his daughter, Antigone. Meanwhile, his sons fight over his throne and try to gain control by influencing Oedipus. But Oedipus leaves the world behind, making his final journey to the Underworld with dignity.

Presentation Suggestions

Place the narrators on one side of the stage. Organize the rest of the characters into two groups. In one group, place Oedipus on a stool with the following characters standing or sitting around him: Laïus, Jocasta, Antigone, Ismene, and Polynices. Place the Oracle on the other stool with the following characters standing or sitting around him: Sphinx, Tiresias, Villager, Theseus, and Creon.

Props

Laïus, Jocasta, Oedipus, and Theseus can be dressed in royal clothing. Ismene, Antigone, and Polynices can be dressed in traveling clothes. The oracle can wear black robes, with stars and moons decorating the robes. The other characters can be dressed in simple clothing.

Delivery Suggestions

The characters should practice their parts so that they can convey the appropriate emotion. Oedipus ages throughout the story, and his voice could reflect this process. He should sound particularly desperate when he discovers the various prophecies and then resigned to his fate at the end.

Characters

- 回 Narrator 1
- 回 Laïus
- 回 Oracle
- 回 Narrator 2
- 回 Jocasta
- 回 Oedipus
- 回 Sphinx
- 回 Tiresias
- 回 Villager
- 回 Antigone
- 回 Ismene
- 回 Theseus
- 回 Creon
- 回 Polynices

OEDIPUS

Narrator 1: The story of Oedipus starts before he was born. King Laïus of Thebes and his wife, Jocasta, longed to have a child. After many years had passed, King Laïus consulted the oracle of Apollo at Delphi to learn if he would ever have an heir.

Laïus: I have been married to Jocasta for many years, but we have not been blessed with a child. Can you tell me if we will ever be granted our fondest desire?

Oracle: You will have a son, Laïus.

Laïus: That is wonderful news!

Oracle: Wait, there is more that you should know. Do you remember when you carried off King Pelops's son?

Laïus: I was young, and that was a foolish act I've come to regret.

Oracle: As well you should, for Pelops cursed you—and Zeus heard his curse. You will have a son, but you will lose your life at his hand.

Narrator 2: Laïus knew he had wronged Pelops and believed the oracle's prophecy. He decided to leave Jocasta, but after a long time, their love over-powered them. Before long, Jocasta gave birth to a son.

Jocasta: What can we do, Laïus? What kind of life does our child face if he will be driven to so desperate an act?

Laïus: I don't know what we can do, unless we spare all of us years of grief and end his life before he can become so miserable at our hands.

Jocasta: I can't bear the thought of losing him, but I also can't imagine life without you.

Laïus: I'll come up with a plan for the baby. I'm sorry that we're all suffering for my earlier acts.

Narrator 1: Laïus called a shepherd and instructed him to bind the child with a thong and leave him in the mountains to die. Instead, the shepherd gave him to a friend who was a servant to the Polybus, king of Corinth. King Polybus and his wife, Merope, raised the child as their own, making him their heir.

Because his feet were swollen from being bound at the ankles with the thong, they named him Oedipus, which meant "swollen foot."

Narrator 2: Oedipus had a happy childhood until one evening at a banquet an envious citizen taunted him, claiming that he was not the king's true son. Oedipus asked his parents, and they calmed him while avoiding the truth. Oedipus continued to fret over the revelation and consulted the oracle of Delphi, hoping to learn that the citizen's statement was a lie.

Oedipus: I have heard terrible rumors about my parentage. Can you reveal the truth about my father and mother to me?

Oracle: There is a prophecy that is indeed disturbing.

Oedipus: I must know the truth! Tell me.

Oracle: It has been decreed that you shall slay your father.

Oedipus: How can that be? I love my father.

Oracle: That may be, but the future cannot be altered. And there is more that you need to know.

Oedipus: Nothing you could tell me could be more distressing than being told I would one day kill my father.

Oracle: Don't speak hastily, Oedipus. Not only will you kill your father, but you will also marry your mother. You will have children together, but they will not be welcome additions to the world.

Oedipus: I must leave immediately. I can't let this happen.

Narrator 1: Oedipus immediately left on the road to Boeotia. Near Delphi, he met a chariot carrying an old man and several servants. They filled the road, refusing to give way to allow Oedipus to pass easily. Distraught from the prophecies, Oedipus had little patience. He tried to push his way through, but the servants pushed back, and a fight ensued. Enraged by the affront, Oedipus killed the old man and all but one of the servants. The remaining servant escaped, taking refuge in a distant part of the country. Oedipus continued on his journey. He had no idea that the man he had killed was King Laïus and that he had fulfilled the first part of the prophecy.

Narrator 2: After some time, Oedipus arrived at the city of Thebes, where he discovered that the seven gates were closed. A winged sphinx, which had the shape of maiden in the front and a lion in the back, had settled on a cliff outside the city wall. She had learned a variety of riddles from the Muses, and she forced every passerby to try to answer a riddle. If the person failed, the sphinx would tear the hapless traveler's body to pieces. King Creon decreed that whoever could answer a riddle and rid them of the sphinx could marry his sister Jocasta and take the throne of the dead king. Oedipus decided he had little to lose, so he accepted the challenge and climbed the cliff.

Oedipus: I am here to answer a riddle! Give me your best one!

Sphinx: You're a confident young man, but you'll soon regret this.

Oedipus: That may be, but I have little to lose.

Sphinx: Here is the riddle then. In the morning it goes on four feet. At noon it goes on two feet. In the evening it goes on three feet. It is the only creature that changes the number of its feet. What is it?

Oedipus: It is man. In the morning of his life, when he is a weak helpless child, he crawls on his two hands and two feet. At the noon of his life, when he is strong, he walks on two feet. And in the evening of his life, he leans on his third foot, a staff, as he moves along.

Narrator 1: The sphinx screamed in frustration and threw herself to the rocks below. The gates of Thebes opened, and the citizens rushed out to thank Oedipus. He was taken to meet Jocasta and decided that, although she was somewhat older than he, a marriage seemed acceptable. They had four children together, twin boys called Eteocles and Polynices, and two daughters, Antigone and Ismene.

Narrator 2: After some time, a plague of pestilence hit the land, and the people asked Oedipus to discover why they were once again under siege. Oedipus called for Tiresias, a blind seer, to help determine what he should do.

Tiresias: Oh King, let me go. Don't ask me to reveal what I know. It will only bring tragedy to you.

Oedipus: That's not an answer. You're evading me. Tell me the truth.

Tiresias: The truth will not serve anyone well.

Oedipus: Were you involved in this tragedy? Is that why you refuse to answer me? Is this your fault?

Tiresias: Don't speak to me like that. *You* are the evil that taints the city. You murdered the king, and now you live an unholy life.

Oedipus: You're talking nonsense! Are you a soothsayer or a trickster?

Tiresias: You need only open your eyes, and you'll see that what you've done is evil.

Narrator 1: Oedipus sent Tiresias away, trying to reconcile what he said with what he knew. When he told Jocasta what Tiresias said, she was outraged at the accusation.

Jocasta: These prophets know nothing. Did I ever tell you that an oracle told my first husband Laïus that he would die at the hands of his son. But our son was left to die in the mountains, and a robber killed Laïus. Some prophecy that was!

Oedipus: Is this true? How old was Laïus when he was killed? What did he look like?

Jocasta: He was tall, and his hair was just turning white. Actually, he looked something like you.

Oedipus: Tiresias was right! He knows the truth! I did kill my father.

Jocasta: What are you talking about, Oedipus? King Polybus died of old age. You're frightening me!

Narrator 2: Oedipus knew in his heart that the prophecy had come true, but he sent for the servant that had witnessed King Laïus's death. The servant, who had been living in exile, confirmed Oedipus's role in the king's death. Then Oedipus learned that king Laïus and Jocasta had indeed abandoned him as a babe.

Narrator 1: Oedipus was so distressed that he planned to kill Jocasta and then take his own life. But before he could enact this terrible deed, Jocasta hanged herself above her bed. Oedipus tore the clasps from her robe and used them to pierce his eyes so he could never again see what he had done. A blind and broken man, he left Thebes, wandering with his daughter Antigone, who guided him on his way.

Narrator 2: He journeyed to the oracle of Pythian Apollo, knowing he had to atone for his acts. The oracle told him that his punishment would not be eternal—no one could have tried harder to avoid his fate. Oedipus and Antigone continued their wanderings until he came upon a villager from Colonus.

Oedipus: Where are we, sir?

Villager: You are in the grove of the Furies, in Colonus.

Oedipus: Who is your ruler?

Villager: Our king is Theseus. Haven't you heard of him? He's famous throughout the land.

Oedipus: Can you take a message to him? Please be my messenger and beg him to come here. Tell him that it's a small favor and that it will bring him great reward.

Villager: What can a blind man give to a noble king? You seem sincere, however. I shall do as you say. Stay here and I'll let our king decide what to do.

Narrator 1: While Oedipus waited, he prayed to the Furies, asking them to show him the course ahead. Before long, the village elders arrived, fearing that this old, blind man would bring the wrath of the Furies on their village. Antigone begged for compassion.

Antigone: Please let us stay. Look at my father. He is old and troubled in spirit. He offers no threat to you. Grant us your favor, so that he can find peace again.

Narrator 2: While the elders discussed what to do, a girl seated on a small horse approached with a servant behind.

Antigone: Father, it's my sister Ismene! She must be bringing us news from home.

Ismene: Father, Sister, I bring terrible news from home. Eteocles and Polynices are fighting to control the throne. First Polynices took his turn, but Eteocles would not wait for his own turn. He caused a revolt among the people, and Polynices was banished.

Antigone: Where is Polynices now?

Ismene: Rumor has it he's in Argos. We've heard he married the daughter of King Adrastus. He is preparing to return to avenge himself on Eteocles and capture the throne. The King is said to have committed seven armies to the battle.

Oedipus: This is dreadful. I must stop this.

Antigone: Is there anything else we should know, Ismene?

Ismene: Yes, I'm afraid there is. A new oracle was proclaimed. The decree is that the sons of King Oedipus can do nothing without their father, whether dead or alive. They are desperately searching for you.

Oedipus: So now I am needed, is that right? An old, blind man?

Ismene: Father, you know you are needed. Our uncle Creon is coming here in search of you. I hurried to get here ahead of him because he is coming to try to convince you to take Eteocles's side.

Oedipus: It is clear that I must stay alive so I can resolve this. Neither of my sons is worthy of the throne. Only my daughters deserve to rule!

Narrator 1: Oedipus's wise observations and kingly demeanor impressed the elders who had been listening. They urged Theseus to meet with him, and Theseus approached Oedipus with compassion.

Theseus: Oedipus, I know who you are, and I have heard of your fate. You have suffered grievously, and your misfortunes move me. Tell me why you wish to speak with me. I am prepared to help you with whatever resources I have at hand.

Oedipus: I see that you are a noble soul, and I have come asking if you will accept my body as my gift to you. If you accept and bury me, you will receive a rich reward for your kindness.

Theseus: This doesn't make sense. I can do much more than bury you in my country.

Oedipus: It's not as simple a request as it may seem. You see, you will have to wage a war to get this body. My sons are fighting for the throne, and I need to gain control of the situation before I have my final peace.

Theseus: The gods have guided you to me, and it will be my honor to help you in this task. There is no need for you to trouble yourself. I recommend that you make yourself comfortable in my palace and let me take up your fight.

Oedipus: I accept your gracious offer with humility and gratitude.

Narrator 2: Theseus left to begin his quest. While Oedipus took his rest, Creon, King of Thebes came to Colonus with armed warriors and sought out Oedipus. He pretended to be sympathetic to Oedipus.

Creon: Oedipus, I have heard of the terrible path you've been forced to take. Let me take you back to Thebes. I offer my escort and my protection.

Oedipus: I have no intention of leaving.

Creon: But your wise counsel is needed. Everyone in Thebes would welcome you.

Oedipus: Do you think I am a fool? You come seeking me only for your own benefit. I shall not go with you, and my sons shall see no more of Thebes than what they need for burial.

Narrator 1: The citizens of Colonus ensured that Creon could not carry off Oedipus, but Creon issued orders to capture Antigone and Ismene. The warriors successfully dragged them away while Creon taunted Oedipus.

Creon: I may not have you, Oedipus, but I have what you value most—your daughters! You can continue your wanderings alone!

Narrator 2: Just then, Theseus returned, having heard of Creon's arrival. He sent soldiers to bring back the young women and told Creon he would be detained until the daughters returned safely.

Creon: Theseus, you misunderstand. I didn't come to make trouble with you. I had no idea this blind, old man meant anything to you. I didn't think your country wanted to shelter a man who had married his mother and killed his father.

Theseus: Quiet! You better hope that his daughters return safely.

Narrator 1: Soon the soldiers brought Antigone and Ismene back. In the meantime, word came to Oedipus that Polynices had arrived in Colonus, asking to meet with Oedipus.

Oedipus: Polynices deserves nothing but my scorn. I won't even talk to him.

Antigone: Father, shouldn't you at least hear what he has to say? Perhaps there's something we should know before you pass judgment on him.

Oedipus: I'll honor your request, daughter, but I am going to ask Theseus to provide me with guards. I just don't trust him.

Narrator 2: Polynices arrived with tears in his eyes and threw himself at his father's feet.

Polynices: Father, what has happened to you? May the gods forgive me for wronging you so grievously. Can you forgive me, Father? Please speak to me.

Antigone: Polynices, tell us what brings you here. Perhaps that will encourage Father to speak with you.

Polynices: After Eteocles took the throne and drove me out of Thebes, I was taken in by the king of Argos, Adrastus. I married his daughter, and Adrastus's allies became my allies. With their help, I can restore you to the throne. Father, let me give you back your rightful crown.

Oedipus: You expect me to believe you after what you've done? You drove me from the land. You put this beggar's cloak on my back. If you'd had your way, I'd be dead long ago. You and your brother will fall in your own blood. Take that reply back to your allies.

Antigone: Polynices, please go back to Argos. Don't fight any more. Let Eteocles keep the throne and live in peace.

Polynices: I can't leave this unresolved. If I flee, I'll be disgraced.

Narrator 1: Oedipus had decided to leave his sons' fate to the gods and resisted his children's pleas. As thunder rolled above, he called for Theseus to escort him to a place where he could die in peace without any witnesses. The citizens who had come to admire him and his daughter followed him along part of his route. During the last part of his journey, he suddenly found the strength to see and walk proudly.

Narrator 2: Oedipus walked to a cave in the grove of the Erinyes, where he bathed and donned a fine robe provided by his daughters. He kissed his daughters farewell.

Oedipus: Now my beloved children, I must leave you. Remember that I love you and wish you long and happy lives. Now, turn away, so that I can leave in peace. Theseus, thank you for kindness. Please care for my daughters.

Narrator 1: Theseus accompanied Oedipus to the opening to the cave, which led to the Underworld. The Earth stood still as the Underworld reverently opened its doors to accept King Oedipus. Finally free from pain and regret, Oedipus left Earth forever.

ORPHEUS AND EURYDICE

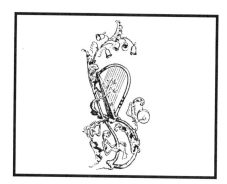

Orpheus was the son of Apollo and Calliope, one of the nine Muses. A fine musician, Orpheus wandered the mountains and woodland, singing with his lyre. He fell in love with Eurydice and married her, only to lose her to a poisonous snakebite. In his grief, Orpheus searched until he found the entrance to the Underworld, where his music softened the hearts of all who heard it. Hades told him that Eurydice could return to Earth if Orpheus trusted him and didn't look back as they made their way back to Earth. Orpheus began to doubt that Eurydice was behind him and looked back just before making it to freedom. Later the nymphs of Thrace killed Orpheus because he wouldn't dance with them. At last he was reunited with Eurydice in the Underworld.

Presentation Suggestions

The narrators, Hades, and Persephone can sit on stools on one side. Orpheus and Eurydice can stand in the center. Mnemosyne, Calliope, and Apollo can sit on stools on the other side.

Props

The characters can wear robes consistent with the dress of gods and goddesses. Add a lyre and flutes to the stage if possible. To involve other characters, consider having nine girls dress up as the nine Muses, each one holding an instrument, a pen, a book, and so forth to represent their gifts.

Delivery Suggestions

Orpheus should sound desperate and grieving after he loses Eurydice. Eurydice should sound frightened when bitten and desperate when Orpheus looks back at her while leaving the Underworld.

Characters

- ◙ Narrator 1
- ◙ Mnemosyne
- ◙ Narrator 2
- ◙ Calliope
- ◙ Apollo
- ◙ Orpheus
- ◙ Eurydice
- ◙ Hades
- ◙ Persephone

ORPHEUS AND EURYDICE

Narrator 1: Zeus and the Titaness Mnemosyne had nine daughters, who were called the Muses. Mnemosyne spent many hours telling them wondrous tales of the Olympians.

Mnemosyne: My daughters, each of you will have a special gift. Calliope, you have the gift of poetry. Clio, you have the gift of history. Polyhymnia, the gift of sacred songs is yours. Urania, you will know all of astronomy. Erato, your gift is that of lyric choral poetry. Thalia, your good nature shows that you have the gift of comedy. Terpsichore, you will be forever admired for your dance. Melpomene, your gift of tragedy will be ever memorable. And Euterpe will shine through her gift of playing the flute. Now, my daughters, listen to these stories. Each of you will help share these stories through your music, dance, and drama.

Narrator 2: Mnemosyne shared all she knew with the Muses, and they turned the stories into poetry, dance, and song. Apollo participated in their choral training, teaching them to sing together harmoniously. The Muses created the seven-tone musical scale, based on the seven spheres.

Narrator 1: It was not surprising that Apollo fell victim to the charms of one of the Muses. He and Calliope had a son together.

Calliope: Apollo, we have created a talented and beautiful son. He will have great gifts to share with the gods and goddesses. I am calling him Orpheus.

Apollo: Yes, Calliope, I know he will make us all proud. I've brought him a fine gift. It's a lyre with seven strings, each one a pure and sweet sound.

Calliope: Will you teach him to play, Apollo? Orpheus will become a fine musician with your guidance and inspiration.

Narrator 2: Apollo found Orpheus to be an apt and skillful student. Orpheus quickly grew up and charmed the countryside with his playing. Men and women stopped their daily tasks to listen. Tales are told of streams that stopped flowing in amazement at his music. Orpheus wandered the forests and mountains, never fearing the wild animals. His music held all who heard him play in thrall.

Narrator 1: Even the nymphs of streams and woodland, called Dryads, came to listen to Orpheus. It was not surprising that he fell in love with Eurydice, an especially sweet, lovely nymph. When Eurydice's and Orpheus's eyes met, they were filled with love for each other.

Orpheus: What is your name?

Eurydice: I am Eurydice. I know that you are Orpheus. Your reputation as a fine musician is known to all of us.

Orpheus: Will you walk with me?

Eurydice: Of course, if you'll play your lyre for me.

Narrator 2: Soon Orpheus and Eurydice married, but their happiness was short lived. Eurydice was dancing in the meadow with the other Dryads when Aristaeus tried to seize her for himself. She ran from him, stepping on a snake.

Eurydice: Orpheus! I've been bitten!

Narrator 1: Orpheus rushed to her side, but the poison worked quickly, and Eurydice died in his arms. Hermes gently closed her eyes and led her away to the Underworld.

Orpheus: Eurydice, Eurydice! Don't leave me! I can't bear life without you.

Narrator 2: At first, Orpheus couldn't play his lyre. Then he began to think of a plan to get his beloved Eurydice back.

Orpheus: If only I can find you, Eurydice. My music has stopped the streams from flowing. Maybe it will soften the hearts of the gods, and they will return you to me.

Narrator 1: Orpheus played his lyre and lamented through his songs. The gods wept for his loss, but the only ones who could help him were the king and queen of the Underworld, Hades and Persephone. Orpheus began searching for an entrance to Hades so that he could make his appeal.

Narrator 2: At last, Orpheus found his way to the end of the Earth and to the gates of Hades. The three-headed dog, Cerberus, stopped barking at the gate to listen to him. Orpheus's music moved the iron gates to open for him. Orpheus wandered through the Underworld, singing of his lost love.

Orpheus: Listen to my tale, one of truth and sadness. I have come of my own free will to this place of darkness and spirits. I don't come to steal or to discover your secrets. I only come to find my beloved. Listen to my songs, and you will know my words are true.

Narrator 1: Orpheus sang with such beauty and grief that every soul stopped to listen. The Erinyes, cruel goddesses who tormented victims in the Underworld, dropped their whips and wept tears of blood. Sisyphus was allowed to rest the stone that he pushed uphill eternally. The wheel to which Ixion was tied for his torture stopped for a time.

Hades: Persephone, Orpheus sounds truly tortured.

Persephone: Perhaps we should let Eurydice go.

Hades: But we have never let someone leave our kingdom.

Persephone: Listen to him. His grief is so strong that he risked coming here. His loss tortures him.

Hades: All right, call him to me, but he must earn the right to have her.

Persephone: Orpheus, come and listen to Hades. He has an offer for you.

Hades: Your music has moved me. I have a plan. I will release Eurydice, but you must go first. She will follow behind, but you must not turn and look at her. You must trust that she'll be there. If you break that trust with one look—just a single glance—she will remain here forever. Can you agree to these terms?

Orpheus: Of course! I will do anything to rescue my beloved.

Hades: Then be on your way. But heed my words, Orpheus. Trust me and do not look back.

Narrator 2: Orpheus started up the dark path, joyful at the reunion ahead. But the way was long. It became dark and threatening. Orpheus began to doubt that Eurydice was still behind him. His fear overtook him—and he looked back.

Eurydice: Orpheus, the Fates are calling me back to the Underworld. Save me, Orpheus. I can't resist their call. Good-bye, my beloved Orpheus.

Narrator 1: Eurydice was lost to Orpheus once again. He raged against the gods and resumed his wandering. He began singing again, hoping that those in the Underworld would give him another chance. But his entreaties were ignored.

Narrator 2: In his wanderings, Orpheus again came upon the Thracian nymphs. They urged him to forget Eurydice and sing of joy again. Orpheus repulsed them, and his rebuffs angered the nymphs so much that they sought revenge. They tore him to pieces and threw his body into the river. Orpheus's head floated alongside his lyre. When his head reached the island of Lesbos, the Muses buried him, sending his lyre to the heavens to a place among the stars.

Narrator 1: At last Orpheus and Eurydice were united in the Underworld, where they walked among the dead, together for all eternity.

PAN

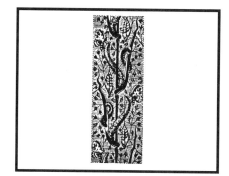

The legend of Pan appears in every region of Greece. The Centaur Chiron raised Pan, who protected flocks and agriculture. Although Pan is generally thought to be the son of Hermes, the identity of his mother varies. In some stories, he falls in love with Eurydice, the wife of Orpheus. In this script, Pan seeks love with Pitys, Echo, and Syrinx, failing with all three.

Presentation Suggestions

The narrators should sit on either side of the stage. Hermes, Zeus, and Hera should stand to one side. Pan should be in the center, and Pitys, Echo, and Syrinx should stand on the other side.

Props

Hermes, Zeus, and Hera can wear regal clothing. Pan should look rugged, with ragged fur hanging from his clothes to look like a goat's hide. Pitys, Echo, and Syrinx could be dressed in simple dresses. The background can look like a woodland setting, with rocky hills in the background.

Delivery Suggestions

Hermes, Zeus, and Hera should sound powerful. Pan should sound eager to find a nymph to love. Pitys and Syrinx should sound anxious to escape Pan. Echo should speak quickly, like a chatterbox.

Characters

- ◉ Narrator 1
- ◉ Narrator 2
- ◉ Hermes
- ◉ Zeus
- ◉ Pan
- ◉ Pitys
- ◉ Hera
- ◉ Echo
- ◉ Syrinx

PAN

Narrator 1: Pan, the son of Hermes and a nymph, was not a handsome god. When he was born, he was so ugly that his mother ran away screaming. It's not surprising that she ran away. He was born with goat's legs, horns, and a coat of shaggy hair.

Narrator 2: But his father was not distressed by Pan's unusual looks. He took him to Olympus so the other gods could meet him. They found him amusing and enjoyed his unusual appearance.

Hermes: Look at my son! Is he not a wonder?

Zeus: We need to find something for his to do, Hermes. What do you propose?

Hermes: He seems well suited to be outdoors. Look at those legs!

Zeus: True, with those legs and hooves, he could cross the hills of Greece with ease. Hermes, Pan will be in charge of nature. He can protect hunters, shepherds, and all who pass their days in nature.

Narrator 1: Pan usually was quite happy with his life. He would watch over the shepherds and their flocks, dancing through the night among the nymphs.

Narrator 2: But on occasion, loneliness and despair at his ugliness would overcome him. He would sulk in his cave, and if a shepherd or weary traveler happened to come near, his screams would terrify them. Even today, when someone is frightened. he is said to be in a panic, so named after Pan's terrorizing.

Narrator 1: One day, Pan talked with his father.

Pan: Father, I am lonely and want to find a companion.

Hermes: Pan, just look around you. There are nymphs everywhere. Surely one will suit you.

Pan: I'll keep looking, Father, but I'm not encouraged. They all run away in fear.

Narrator 2: But eventually Pan fell in love with the nymph Pitys. Unfortunately, Boreas, the North Wind, also loved Pitys.

Pan: Pitys, come away with me. Let me show you my enduring love.

Pitys: Pan, I do love you, but Boreas loves me, too. I'm afraid to cross him. He is a jealous god, and his revenge can be cruel.

Pan: Don't worry about him, Pitys. Come away with me! We can hide from him in the cave and dance through the woods at night.

Pitys: All right, Pan, but we must be careful.

Narrator 1: But Boreas did seek revenge. He blew through the woods, grabbed Pitys, and threw her against a rock. Her limbs were crushed, but Gaea took pity on her and transformed her into a pine tree.

Narrator 2: Pan also fell in love with the nymph Echo. But she talked so much that Pan could never properly court her. One day, Hera suspected that Zeus was playing with the nymphs, and she came down from Olympus to look for him.

Hera: Echo, have you seen Zeus?

Echo: No, Hera. Why would I see Zeus? He's too important a god for me to ever see. I haven't seen him for a long time. I know he couldn't be doing anything here. After all, he's too powerful to worry about nymphs like us. . . .

Hera: Echo, stop rattling on and think a minute. Have you seen Zeus?

Echo: No, Hera. Why would I see Zeus? He's too important a god for me to ever see. I haven't seen him for a long time. I know he couldn't be doing anything here. After all, he's too powerful to worry about nymphs like us. . . .

Narrator 1: Hera couldn't bear listening to her chatter.

Hera: Echo, you have angered me with your pointless prattle. From now on, you will not be able to form your own words. You will only be able to repeat the words another has said. That is your punishment for trying to protect Zeus.

Narrator 2: Pan overheard this and thought he could at last win Echo's heart. After all, he only needed to say, "I love you," and she would have to echo his words. She would be his! But before he could carry out his plan, she fell in love with Narcissus.

Narrator 1: Narcissus was so handsome that everyone who met him fell in love with him. But Narcissus was only enchanted with himself. Echo followed him as he hunted in the woods, hoping for a loving word that she could repeat to him. Finally, Narcissus bent down to drink from a pool of water one evening.

He looked at his face reflected in the water and became entranced. He said those three magic words, but to his own image. Echo finally had her chance to show her love as she repeated his words.

Echo: I love you.

Narrator 2: But Narcissus was so hypnotized by his own image that he didn't hear her. He sat for so long, staring at himself, that he wasted away and died. Hermes led him to the Underworld, and a narcissus flower grew where he died.

Narrator 1: Echo stood nearby, grieving until she faded away, leaving only her voice to endlessly repeat other's words through eternity.

Narrator 2: Some time later, Pan saw the nymph Syrinx and fell instantly in love with her. But his strange appearance terrified her, and she ran away.

Pan: Syrinx, stop! I only want to get to know you.

Syrinx: Leave me alone, Pan. I don't want anything to do with you.

Narrator 1: Syrinx ran and ran, with Pan right behind her.

Syrinx: Go away, Pan! I can't bear to look on you.

Pan: Just stop for a moment! I won't hurt you!

Narrator 2: Syrinx did stop, but only to pray to her father, the river god.

Syrinx: Father, save me! Keep me from Pan! Change me into anything—even the reeds in the river!

Narrator 1: Her father granted Syrinx's prayer and changed her into a reed. Pan wandered through the reeds looking for her.

Pan: Syrinx, where are you? Speak to me, please.

Narrator 2: But the reeds all swayed together, and Pan couldn't identify Syrinx.

Narrator 1: Finally, Pan consoled himself by cutting ten reeds of different lengths. He lashed them together and played tunes on them, calling them his syrinx. For eternity, Pan wandered through the hills and woods, playing his pipes, thinking of his beloved syrinx. And if you go to Greece, you may hear him playing even today.

PERSEUS

King Danaüs had fifty daughters, but he didn't want them to marry King Aegyptus's fifty sons. When forced into the marriages, he counseled his daughters to kill their husbands. All Danaüs's daughters followed his directive—except Hypermnestra, who fell in love with Lynceus. Many years later, they became rulers of Argos. In time, their grandson, Acrisius, took over the throne. He learned from an oracle that his grandson would eventually kill him. To avoid this fate, Acrisius imprisoned his daughter, Danaë, but Zeus visited the beautiful girl, and she bore him a child, Perseus.

Acrisius sent Danaë and Perseus to sea in a chest, assuming they would drown. But Zeus intervened, and they landed safely on an island, where an elderly fisherman, Dictys, befriended them. As Danaë raised Perseus, King Polydectes decided he wanted to marry her. But Danaë refused, and Perseus promised to protect her. King Polydectes knew he had to get rid of Perseus. He sent him away to bring back the head of the terrible Gorgon Medusa. Various gods helped Perseus as he used magic and trickery to find the Gorgons and then cut off Medusa's head. On his return, he rescued Andromeda from a vicious sea monster. They married and returned to Argos, assuming that Acrisius would welcome him as the hero he had become. Instead, Acrisius fled, afraid his grandson would kill him. Perseus was left to rule the land, becoming a beloved ruler. An excellent athlete, he also participated in many athletic games. During a discus throw, the wind carried the discus off course, and it struck and killed Acrisius, who had returned to Argos and was watching the game. The oracle's prophecy had been fulfilled.

Presentation Suggestions

Place the narrators on stools on the right and left sides of the stage. The following characters should sit on chairs: King Aegyptus, King Danaüs, Acrisius, and the oracle. The following characters should sit in a row behind the others on stools: Zeus, Danaë, Dictys, and Polydectes. The following characters should stand in the back row: Perseus, Athena, Sister, and Andromeda. Alternatively, have everyone stand in rows, with the first set leaving after their lines, and so forth.

Props

      The characters can dress in robes or clothing appropriate to their roles. The items used by Perseus can decorate the stage: shield, sword, and bag. Consider creating a mural that shows statues of people turned to stone, of the islands, and so forth.

Delivery Suggestions

      The characters can use normal voices appropriate to their lines and the action of the script.

Characters

- ▣ Narrator 1
- ▣ King Aegyptus
- ▣ King Danaüs
- ▣ Narrator 2
- ▣ Acrisius
- ▣ Oracle
- ▣ Zeus
- ▣ Danaë
- ▣ Dictys
- ▣ Polydectes
- ▣ Perseus
- ▣ Athena
- ▣ Sister
- ▣ Andromeda

PERSEUS

Narrator 1: The Muses sang the praises of King Danaüs, a mortal who was the first of a line of kings from Libya. King Danaüs had fifty daughters, and, of course, he needed to find fifty husbands for them. His brother, King Aegyptus, had a plan.

King Aegyptus: Brother, I have a solution to the problem for finding husbands for your daughters. It is obvious that my fifty sons should marry your daughters. Everyone will be happy then, and we will have wonderful grandchildren.

King Danaüs: Ah, that would be fine for your sons, but they are not the refined gentlemen I want for my daughters. You needn't concern yourself with my daughters. I'll find husbands for them somehow.

King Aegyptus: Nonsense. Why do you worry about your daughters? You have so many of them! You should be relieved that I am willing to have my sons take them off your hands.

Narrator 2: But King Danaüs did not want his daughters carried off by these ruffians. He secretly built a ship with fifty oars and slipped away, with his daughters pulling at the oars. They fled Libya, landing in Argos. When the people saw this amazing ship, they decided Danaüs was sent to be their king.

Narrator 1: Danaüs proved worthy of their respect, ruling peacefully and kindly. But the peace was shattered when another ship arrived. King Aegyptus's fifty sons had also rowed to Argos.

King Aegyptus: My brother, you can't escape again. Give in gracefully and let my sons marry your daughters. Look at the dynasty we will create!

King Danaüs: It seems you give me no choice. I'll prepare the wedding feast, and we'll celebrate together.

Narrator 2: But King Danaüs had other secret plans, which he made clear to his daughters before the wedding.

King Danaüs: My daughters, I fear that marriage to these men will lead to lives of misery. Therefore I am giving each of you an important gift—a dagger. Kill your husband as soon as you are alone. Don't think about this. Just save yourselves.

Narrator 1: The weddings proceeded, and soon the couples were alone. Forty-nine of the brides followed their father's directive and used their daggers to kill their husbands. But Hypermnestra had immediately fallen in love with her husband, Lynceus. Instead of killing him, they ran away together.

Narrator 2: King Danaüs was left with forty-nine widowed daughters. He tried to find husbands for them, but no men would marry them for fear that the king's daughters would murder any men they married. The Danaïdes, as they came to be known, lived unhappy lives. When they died, they were sent to the Underworld, where they were punished for the murders of their husbands. Each of them was ordered to fill a bath to wash off their sins. But they had to carry water in sieves, and they spent eternity trying to fulfill their sentence.

Narrator 1: King Danaüs grew very old. In need of an heir to his throne, he was compelled to send for Hypermnestra and Lynceus, who had found happiness together.

King Danaüs: Hypermnestra and Lynceus, you must take over the throne when I die. I am happy to see that you have a son who will carry on the rule of this family.

Narrator 2: Reunited with her father, Hypermnestra and Lynceus prepared to take over the throne. They ruled until their deaths, and their son then inherited the throne. When the next in line, Acrisius, inherited the throne, he had no son, but one beautiful daughter, Danaë. Acrisius desperately wanted a son to inherit the throne and went to an oracle to seek advice.

Acrisius: Please, wise one, I have come seeking advice.

Oracle: Explain your problem, my son.

Acrisius: I have no son to inherit the throne. My daughter is beautiful and loving, but she should not be the ruler. What can I do?

Oracle: You will not have a son, I fear. I do see something of great importance in your future, however.

Acrisius: What do you see? Tell me.

Oracle: It's dangerous to look too far ahead. Are you sure you want to know?

Acrisius: Of course! What is it?

Oracle: Your daughter will have a child. This child will grow to be very powerful and one day will kill you.

Acrisius: Then I must ensure that she never weds.

Oracle: You should heed my warning, but I see no change in your future.

Narrator 1: Fearing for his life, Acrisius put Danaë in a chamber with no windows or doors. The only opening was in the roof. No one could see Danaë's beauty, so Acrisius thought he would be safe.

Narrator 2: Alas, Acrisius forgot that Zeus missed very little. Indeed, Zeus spied Danaë from above and was enchanted with her beauty. A master of shape changing, he turned himself into a golden shower and descended through the opening in the roof of the chamber.

Zeus: Danaë, you are too beautiful to be so lonesome. Let me keep you company and make you happy.

Danaë: I have been lonely locked away in this room. I welcome you here for as long as you can stay.

Narrator 1: Zeus made Danaë his bride, and before long she gave birth to their child. When Acrisius heard the cries of a newborn, he broke through the walls in a rage.

Acrisius: What have you done, Danaë? You can't keep this child! Give him to me!

Danaë: Father, this is Zeus's son, whom I have named Perseus. Do you dare to harm him?

Acrisius: I won't hurt him, but I won't keep either of you here now that you've betrayed me. Come with me to the sea.

Narrator 2: Acrisius put Danaë and Perseus in a chest and pushed it into the sea.

Acrisius: This breaks my heart, but when they drown, Poseidon will take the blame instead of me.

Narrator 1: Once again, Acrisius acted without taking Zeus's powers into consideration. Zeus gently steered the chest to an island, where an old fisherman named Dictys hauled in the chest along with his net full of fish.

Dictys: What is this in my nets? It looks like a chest. Perhaps there's a treasure inside.

Danaë: Please help us! We're locked inside the chest!

Dictys: Gods be praised! Someone's alive in there!

Narrator 2: Dictys opened the chest, lifting up the child Danaë offered him.

Dictys: How did you come to be locked in a chest, my dear?

Danaë: My father wanted to keep me from all men, so he locked me in a chamber with only an opening in the ceiling.

Dictys: But why did he punish you so? What had you done?

Danaë: I hadn't done anything. But he desperately feared my having a child.

Dictys: But what harm could a child do to him?

Danaë: It had been foretold that one day his grandchild would end my father's life. He thought he was keeping himself safe. But Zeus made me his bride, and Perseus is our son. Father dared not kill Zeus's son, so he sent us away in this chest, perhaps hoping Poseidon would do what he could not.

Dictys: You're both safe now. You have landed on the island of Seriphus, a fine place to live. Come with me to my humble home. I have little, but I'll share it with you and help you stay safe while you raise your son.

Narrator 1: Danaë lovingly raised her son to be a fine young man. She remained faithful in memory to Zeus, but she attracted the eye of Polydectes, the king of Seriphus. Polydectes visited Danaë.

Polydectes: Danaë, I have an offer for you.

Danaë: Sir, what is your pleasure?

Polydectes: Your lovely nature and beautiful form have held my attention for many years. I want a wife and have chosen you for that great honor.

Danaë: Surely you know that I'm married to Zeus! I can't marry you.

Polydectes: You think you won't, but one day I'll find you alone and carry you away. You'll become my bride, just as I desire. And if you resist, there's are other ways to persuade you. Tell me, Danaë, just how much do you love your son?

Narrator 2: Perseus overheard the conversation and never left his mother's side in fear that Polydectes would carry through with his threats to abduct Danaë.

Narrator 1: Finally, Polydectes pretended that he was going to marry a princess from a neighboring island. It was customary for the men to bring the king a wedding gift. Because Perseus came from a humble home, he had no gift to bring. Instead, he went to see Polydectes with an offer of his services.

Perseus: Polydectes, I come to congratulate you on your forthcoming wedding. As my gift, I offer you my services. I am strong and will not back down from a challenge. What might I do for you?

Narrator 2: Little did Perseus know that Polydectes was hoping for this very opportunity.

Polydectes: Perseus, there is a challenge that I hope you can meet. No one has ever been able to accomplish this task. Are you sure you want to pursue what I am about to request?

Perseus: Sir, I am at your service. What do you desire?

Polydectes: Medusa. Slay the monster and bring me her head as proof that you have succeeded.

Narrator 1: Medusa was one of the three horrible Gorgon sisters. Just looking upon one of the sisters turned any living creature to stone. Polydectes didn't care about getting rid of Medusa; he wanted only to be rid of Perseus. Only then would he have the opportunity to gain the hand of the fair Danaë.

Narrator 2: Perseus set out on his quest, asking for help from Athena along the way. Hermes, the god of travelers, appeared with Athena.

Athena: Hermes and I can help you, but you have many challenges ahead. I am loaning you my shield. Keep it clean and polished. It will serve you well as protection. Hermes is lending you his sword, so strong that it will cut through metal.

Perseus: Thank you for your kindness. These are great gifts.

Athena: But they aren't enough. You need to find the nymphs of the north. They have great magic, and only they can provide you with what you need to succeed.

Perseus: Where do I go? How do I find them?

Athena: They are hidden even from the gods. Only the Graeae sisters know.

Perseus: How do I find them?

Athena: They live in a land far to the west where the sun never shines. Everything is gray as dusk, just like the Graeae sisters. They share a single eye and single tooth, their most prized possessions. Think of how you can turn this to your advantage.

Perseus: Thank you for your kindness and assistance. I will always be in your debt.

Narrator 1: Hermes offered to help Perseus with this next challenge. He tucked Perseus under his arm and sped off to the west. When they arrived, it was just as Athena had described—gray and dreary. The Graeae sisters had gray hair and gray faces. They passed one gray eye around, looking through it in turns. Perseus stood by quietly, blending into the grayness. As one sister passed the eye to another, none could see him. He darted forward and wrested the eye out of the sister's hand.

Perseus: Sisters! I have your eye. You'll only get it back if you tell me the way to the nymphs of the north.

Sister: Give us back the eye! We'll consider your request, but we need to each have a turn to see you first.

Perseus: No, no. You'll simply refuse to help me. I have to know the way to the nymphs.

Sister: How do you know that we'll tell you the truth?

Perseus: You'll tell me the truth because if you don't, I'll be back. There's no way you can keep me from taking your eye again. You should know that now.

Narrator 2: The sisters talked it over and decided they had to tell him the way to the nymphs.

Sister: Do you have a way to travel quickly?

Perseus: Yes, Hermes will help me.

Sister: Then listen well. Fly to the north, beyond the North Wind. Keep flying until you come to where the sun never sets. Once you have traveled that far, the nymphs will find you.

Narrator 2: Hermes and Perseus flew off to the North until they came to the nymphs. Once they heard about Perseus's quest, they lent him a pair of winged sandals, a cap of invisibility, and a magic bag to hold whatever he put into it.

Narrator 1: Now that Perseus had the winged sandals, he no longer needed Hermes. Perseus flew to the west, passing the island of the Gorgons. He knew that if he looked directly at the Gorgons, he would be turned to stone, so he used the polished shield to look at their reflection. He saw the grotesque Gorgon sisters sleeping on the shore. Snakes grew out of their heads, and fangs grew from their evil mouths. Stones of what had once been men foolish enough to gaze upon them surrounded the sisters.

Narrator 2: Perseus flew down and used the sword to quickly cut off Medusa's head. As he flew off, a winged horse, the Pegasus, grew out of Medusa's torso. His frantic neighs woke Medusa's sisters, who began to pursue Perseus. Perseus threw Medusa's head into the magic bag, slipped on his cap of invisibility, and sped away. Unable to see Perseus, the sisters gave up their chase.

Narrator 1: As Perseus flew over Ethiopia, he saw what appeared to be a marble statue chained to a rock by the sea. As he looked closer, he realized that tears seeped down the lovely face of Andromeda. He flew down and tried to free her from her chains.

Andromeda: Stop trying to save me! You'll only lose your life!

Perseus: I can't leave you here like this. Who are you? What has led to your imprisonment?

Andromeda: My name is Andromeda. I'm the daughter of King Cepheus and Queen Cassiopeia. When my mother boasted that she was lovelier than the Nereids were, Poseidon became very angry. He couldn't tolerate a mortal comparing herself to the goddesses of the sea. He sent a sea monster to wreak havoc on the kingdom of Ethiopia.

Perseus: But why are you here? You still haven't explained why you are imprisoned.

Andromeda: My father was forced to sacrifice me to the sea monster. This was the only way to appease Poseidon. When the monster gets hungry enough, it will eat me.

Perseus: Was there no one who would help? You are so beautiful. I can't believe no one came to your rescue.

Andromeda: I was engaged to be married to Phineus, but when he saw what had happened, he ran away. He was afraid.

Perseus: I will save you, and if you'll have me, I'll marry you.

Narrator 2: Before Andromeda could answer, the sea monster reared its ugly head out of the sea. Its mouth opened wide as it reached for Andromeda. Perseus dived at the monster and thrust his sword down its throat. The monster's wails reached to the heavens, and it sank beneath the waves. Its blood filled the sea, and ever after those waters were known as the Red Sea.

Narrator 1: The bellowing of the monster alerted Andromeda's cowardly suitor to the fight. Phineus quickly gathered his soldiers and hastened to claim Andromeda as his bride. Andromeda's parents followed, hoping to find their daughter safe from the sea monster. When Phineus insisted that he was going to carry Andromeda away, Perseus took out his shield, calling out to Andromeda.

Perseus: Andromeda, shield your eyes. Trust me—don't watch until I tell you it's safe!

Narrator 2: Perseus took Medusa's head out of the magic bag, and the men were immediately turned to stone. Sadly, Andromeda's parents had also looked upon the terrible head of the Gorgon. But the gods felt sorry for them and made Cepheus and Cassiopeia constellations in the sky so that they could forever watch the events on Earth. Perseus used his sword to cut Andromeda's chains, and they fled to Seriphus.

Narrator 1: When they arrived, Perseus discovered that Polydectes had tried to abduct Danaë as soon as he had left. Danaë and Dictys were in hiding. Outraged, Perseus went to see the Polydectes.

Perseus: Your majesty, I have fulfilled your request. Here is the head!

Narrator 2: Polydectes was so astonished to see Perseus that he looked directly at Medusa and was turned to stone. His entire court looked on as well, and all were lost. The people rejoiced at the death of the despot, giving Perseus and Andromeda a grand wedding. When Perseus returned the magic items to Athena, he also gave her Medusa's head.

Narrator 1: Now a grand hero, Perseus thought that his grandfather would welcome him back. But when he returned to Argos, he found that Acrisius had fled in terror. Perseus became king of Argos and proved to be a kind and wise ruler.

Narrator 2: Perseus was also a fine athlete, and he often participated in the games held throughout Greece. During the discus throw, a wind came up, and Perseus's discus changed course, killing an elderly man who was watching. Thus, the words of the oracle came true, for the old man was Acrisius.

Narrator 1: Perseus continued to bring glory to Greece. He built the city of Mycenae and had many great descendants. When Perseus and Andromeda died, Zeus honored them by putting them in the sky as constellations.

PROMETHEUS AND PANDORA

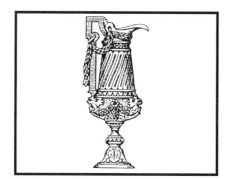

At one time the Titans, powerful giants, fought the Olympian gods. Titan brothers Prometheus and Epimetheus remained loyal to Zeus, who chose to reward them by having them repopulate the Earth. Prometheus took great care in fashioning the mortals, longing to give them comfort and sustenance. Against Zeus's wishes, he gave them fire and meat. After tricking Zeus, Prometheus was sentenced to continued punishment, only to be rescued by Heracles, known to the Latins as Hercules. Woven into this narrative is the story of Pandora, sent by Zeus to further punish the brothers. In this story, Pandora brings along a jug, refusing to heed Zeus's warning to leave it closed. All the plagues of the world are released when she peeks. Only the quality of hope remains for mortals. During the medieval period, the jug was translated as a box, giving us the well-known Pandora's box, which symbolizes the moment when mortals learned of all the world's tragedies.

Presentation Suggestions

The narrators can stand to the sides of the stage. Place Prometheus and Epimetheus in the center, with Zeus and Heracles on one side and Hephaestus and Pandora on the other. Hephaestus and Pandora can enter just before their lines.

Props

The characters can be dressed in gowns or robes. Pandora should wear beautiful clothing, perhaps with flowers or jewels in her hair. Place a jug on the stage.

Delivery Suggestions

Zeus should sound regal and vengeful. Prometheus should sound strong and later resigned to his fate. Pandora should sound sweet and persuasive.

Characters

- ◙ Narrator 1
- ◙ Zeus
- ◙ Epimetheus
- ◙ Prometheus
- ◙ Narrator 2
- ◙ Hephaestus
- ◙ Pandora
- ◙ Heracles

PROMETHEUS AND PANDORA

Narrator 1: The gods frequently waged war, with the unfortunate result that all living creatures on Earth had perished. Zeus decided it was time to restore Earth to its former splendor. He sent for Prometheus and his brother Epimetheus, both Titans, powerful giants who lived on Earth.

Zeus: Prometheus and Epimetheus, I have a task for you.

Epimetheus: What do you need, Zeus?

Zeus: Go down to Earth and fashion new men and beasts.

Prometheus: How will we do this?

Zeus: When you arrive on Earth, simply go to the river. Use the clay on the banks to create the mortals, both human and animal. You'll find it works well. As you work, you can give each creature gifts to make it swift, strong, or whatever traits you see fit to bestow.

Narrator 2: The brothers journeyed to Earth and began to create many creatures. As was his nature, Prometheus took great care, crafting each man in the image of the gods. Epimetheus created the animals, working as quickly as he could.

Epimetheus: Why are you so slow, brother? Look at what I've created in half the time it's taken you to make one mortal.

Prometheus: Good work takes time, Epimetheus. Humans deserve to have the best.

Narrator 1: Unfortunately, Prometheus was so slow that Epimetheus used up all the good gifts on the animals he created. They could run fast, see far, and hear from great distances. They also had warm coats of fur, while the men were left to shiver at night or in the cold. Taking pity on his creations, Prometheus went to Zeus for help.

Prometheus: Zeus, my people are carefully crafted, but they need warmth and a way to prepare their food. Won't you share the sacred fire with them?

Zeus: You must think I'm a fool! Fire is for the gods, not for mere mortals. Get back to your work.

Narrator 2: Prometheus returned to Earth, but he couldn't stop thinking about the fire. He knew he'd probably be punished, but he felt responsible for the creatures he'd created.

Narrator 1: Prometheus sneaked up to Olympus, stole an ember from the fire there, and gave it to man, warning them to never let it die out. The fire not only kept humanity warm, but also kept the beasts at bay. Before long, the humans learned how to kill the beasts and cook their meat. The smell of roasting meat drifted to the heavens, alerting Zeus to Prometheus's betrayal. He summoned Prometheus to his court.

Zeus: You have disobeyed me, Prometheus, but I have a proposal for you. Have the men share with me whatever delicious meats they are preparing. Then perhaps I'll let them keep part of the meat for themselves, along with the fire that you stole from me.

Narrator 2: Prometheus returned to the mortals and gave them careful instructions.

Prometheus: Zeus wants a portion of the meat you are cooking. Here is what I propose. Butcher an ox and divide the meat into two equal portions. Put the fine meat in one sack with the entrails on top. Put the bones in the other sack with the fat on top. Then I'll give Zeus a choice. With some good fortune, he may choose the wrong sack.

Narrator 1: Soon Prometheus returned to Zeus with an invitation.

Prometheus: Zeus, the men have prepared two portions of the ox. You don't have need for all of it, as you said. Why don't you come to Earth and choose your portion? The men can keep the remains.

Narrator 2: Indeed, when Zeus examined the sacks, he assumed that the good meat lay underneath the fat and chose accordingly. He was furious when he realized he'd been duped.

Zeus: Prometheus, you have tricked me for the last time. You are to be bound in chains at the top of the Caucasus Mountains. Every day an eagle will come down from the sky and dine on your liver. By night, your liver will return to health, providing dinner for the eagle the next day. I have another punishment in mind for your precious mortals.

Narrator 1: Until this time, all mortals were men. Zeus decided it was time they had a woman and called Hephaestus to him.

Zeus: Hephaestus, I want you to create a new mortal, fashioned after a goddess rather than a god.

Hephaestus: Do you have anything special in mind for her, Zeus?

Zeus: You can have all the help you need in bestowing gifts on her. Just call on the other gods as you need.

Hephaestus: This will be a worthy project. I can make a wonderful creature, Zeus.

Zeus: But don't make her perfect. The mortals don't deserve perfection!

Hephaestus: I understand, Zeus. You won't be displeased.

Narrator 2: Hephaestus called on the gods and goddesses to help in the creation of the first woman. Aphrodite gave her beauty and charm. Athena taught her cooking, weaving, and spinning. She received many great gifts, but Hephaestus tried to strike a balance, bestowing upon her the gifts of lying and deceit.

Narrator 1: Zeus called Epithemeus to his throne in Olympus.

Epithemeus: Zeus, how can I serve you?

Zeus: Actually, I have a great gift for you. The gods and goddesses have fashioned a woman to be your helpmate on Earth. Her name is Pandora, and you may take her with you on your return. This clay pot is another great gift, but neither you nor Pandora can open it without my permission. Don't defy me.

Narrator 2: Epithemeus was immediately enchanted with Pandora's beauty and skills. Prometheus had warned him to be wary of Zeus's tricks and to refuse any gifts he might offer, but Epithemeus could only gaze on Pandora in wonder. Finally he decided he had to marry her.

Epithemeus: Pandora, I don't want to share you. Zeus has made a gift of you to the mortals, but you will become my bride.

Pandora: I'll be your wife, but I want to find out what is in the clay jar.

Epithemeus: Pandora, you heard what Zeus said. We are to never look inside it without his permission.

Pandora: Surely a little peek won't hurt anything.

Narrator 1: Before Epithemeus could stop her, Pandora broke the seal on the jar and lifted the lid. Out flew all the blessings of the world, returning quickly to the heavens. Following the blessings came the plagues of the world: envy, fear, greed, vanity, old age, sickness, and others.

Narrator 2: Pandora slammed the lid on the jar, but it was too late. The mortals began to suffer these miseries immediately, while Zeus observed in disgust. Only one blessing remained in the pot, and that was hope. That is why today all of mankind has only hope to counter all the challenges they face from birth to death.

Narrator 1: Meanwhile, Prometheus continued to suffer with his continued punishment. Many years later, Heracles passed by while on his quest for the golden apples.

Heracles: Prometheus, why has happened to you?

Prometheus: Zeus is punishing me for giving fire to the mortals.

Heracles: How can your punishment be broken?

Prometheus: It seems I am caught here until someone breaks my chains and takes my place.

Heracles: I can break your chains, and I think I can deliver someone to take your place. But first, let me ensure that that eagle no longer torments you.

Narrator 2: Heracles quickly shot the eagle with his arrow. Known for being the strongest man in the world, he then tore apart the chains. Heracles then brought Chiron the centaur to take Prometheus's place. Prometheus expressed his gratitude to Heracles by telling him not to pick the golden apples on his quest or he would die. Only Atlas could pick these apples of immortality.

Narrator 1: Of course, Zeus observed all that transpired, but he allowed Heracles to free Prometheus. Nevertheless, he had one last punishment. He commanded that Prometheus forever wear an iron ring, complete with a chip from the wall of Caucasus. Prometheus was finally free, but he would always be linked to the mountain.

 # SISYPHUS

Sisyphus, a mortal, was known for his intelligence. The son of Aeolus and a Deucalion, he became the king of Corinth. He outwitted Autolycus, who stole his sheep, by engraving his name on a hoof of each of the sheep. When Zeus stole Aegina, Sisyphus bargained with Aegina's father, trading his knowledge of her whereabouts for fresh water for Corinth. Zeus was not pleased at being found out and punished Sisyphus by sending Thanatos, the spirit of Death, to collect his soul. Once again, Sisyphus used his intelligence, this time capturing Thanatos in chains. With no one dying on Earth, chaos ensued. Finally, Zeus convinced Sisyphus to release Thanatos. Knowing he would be the first soul collected for Hades, Sisyphus had convinced his wife to ignore the usual funeral customs. Sisyphus arrived in the Underworld, complaining about his wife's treatment. Hades sent him back to deal with his wife, and Sisyphus enjoyed a long and happy life. When he finally died of old age, Hermes brought him to Hades, who made him repeatedly push a rock up a steep hill for eternity.

Presentation Suggestions

The narrators should stand to one side of the stage. Autolycus and Asopus can be next and can leave the stage after their lines. Sisyphus should stand in the middle of the stage. Zeus and Hades can stand on the other side of Sisyphus.

Props

Autolycus can be dressed in common clothes. Asopus can be in blue clothes to indicate the river. Sisyphus and Zeus can be dressed in royal clothing. Hades can be dressed in dark clothes.

Delivery Suggestions

Autolycus should sound cunning, pretending to be innocent. Asopus should sound desperate when trying to find his daughter. Sisyphus should sound thoughtful and sincere. Zeus should sound angry. Hades should sound outraged at the behavior of Sisyphus's wife.

Characters

- 回 Narrator 1
- 回 Narrator 2
- 回 Sisyphus
- 回 Autolycus
- 回 Asopus
- 回 Zeus
- 回 Hades

SISYPHUS

Narrator 1: Sisyphus, the son of Aeolus, was a clever mortal. He was a Deucalion and founded Corinth, which was then called Ephyra. He was a strong ruler, always looking for an opportunity to improve his kingdom.

Narrator 2: Sisyphus used his intelligence skillfully. One day he realized that his flock of sheep was missing. Autolycus, the son of Hermes and Chione, had inherited the trait of stealing. Naturally, Sisyphus suspected that Autolycus had stolen the sheep and confronted him.

Sisyphus: Autolycus, you are nothing more than a common thief.

Autolycus: How can you say that, Sisyphus? What have I done to you to anger you so?

Sisyphus: You've stolen my sheep!

Autolycus: Who are you to say these are your sheep? They look like any other sheep that roam the meadows. You'll have a hard time proving these are yours.

Sisyphus: No, you're wrong, Autolycus. I can prove they are *all* mine.

Autolycus: And how will you do that?

Sisyphus: Pick up a front hoof of any of the sheep. There you'll find my name.

Narrator 1: Sisyphus had engraved his name under a front hoof of each sheep. Autolycus had no choice but to return the sheep to Sisyphus.

Narrator 2: One day Sisyphus saw Zeus carrying Aegina, the beautiful daughter of the god of the River Asopus, through the streets of Corinth. Soon he spied Asopus looking for his daughter. Sisyphus began thinking about how Asopus could help him gain fresh water for Corinth. The Corinthians had no water source inside the walls and had to carry the water a long ways. Sisyphus seized this opportunity to strike a bargain.

Sisyphus: Asopus, why are you here in Corinth?

Asopus: I am looking for my daughter, Aegina.

Sisyphus: Perhaps I can help you. But I expect a favor in return.

Asopus: What do you want, Sisyphus?

Sisyphus: It's a simple request. Give my city a fresh-water spring.

Asopus: You know I hate to give away my water.

Sisyphus: I think you'll want to know where your daughter is, Asopus. Decide carefully.

Asopus: All right, you have your spring.

Narrator 1: Asopus struck the ground, and a crystal clear spring bubbled out of the ground.

Asopus: Now tell me where my daughter is.

Sisyphus: Zeus carried her off. They went that way, in a great hurry.

Narrator 2: Asopus pursued his daughter and Zeus in a rage. Soon he caught up to them.

Asopus: Zeus, give me back my daughter!

Narrator 1: Zeus was taken unawares and was not prepared with his usual thunderbolt. He changed himself into a rock and changed Aegina into an island. Sisyphus had gotten his spring. But Asopus had lost his daughter, and Zeus was furious with Sisyphus for telling Asopus where he was. Zeus ordered Thanatos, the winged spirit of death, to his throne.

Zeus: Thanatos, Sisyphus needs to be punished. Collect him and take him to Hades.

Narrator 2: Sisyphus expected Zeus to avenge himself, and had prepared himself. He gathered a long chain and kept it ready. When Thanatos appeared, Sisyphus distracted him with clever talk while Sisyphus wrapped him in chains. Knowing that he couldn't hold Thanatos forever, Sisyphus laid his plans. He secretly enlisted his wife's help, telling her that when he died, she should not pay him the usual funeral honors. She knew that Sisyphus was cleverer than she was, so even though she didn't understand, she reluctantly agreed.

Narrator 1: Meanwhile, with Thanatos in chains, no mortals were dying. The natural order of the world had been disrupted. The elderly, frail, and sick wondered when they would be allowed to rest from their miseries. The healthy began to take risks and act foolishly, knowing they'd live forever. Zeus finally ordered Sisyphus to come to his throne.

Zeus: Sisyphus, you have proven your cleverness, but now this must stop. Hades has received no souls since you tied up Thanatos. Everyone is confused. I'm ordering you to let Thanatos go.

Sisyphus: All right, Zeus. I agree that it's time to let Death return to work.

Narrator 2: Sisyphus released Thanatos, knowing that he would be the first victim Death claimed. But this time Zeus sent Hermes to collect him. His faithful wife remembered her promise and didn't put the usual coin under his tongue or give him a funeral feast. Sisyphus arrived in front of Hades as a poor beggar.

Hades: Sisyphus, why have you come here like this? You were not a poor mortal.

Sisyphus: It was my wife's doing.

Hades: This is unbecoming of a king. Why did she do this?

Sisyphus: This is all I have been thinking about since I died. I feel so betrayed— and I thought she loved me. Perhaps she didn't want to spend the money required for a proper funeral.

Hades: But you were the king! You had adequate wealth for a proper funeral.

Sisyphus: Of course I did, but once dead I have no control over what she does, do I?

Hades: Not from your grave. But I am going to give her a surprise. I'm sending you back so you can punish her for her betrayal.

Narrator 1: Of course, this was exactly what Sisyphus had hoped for, and he returned to his life on Earth. He celebrated with his beloved wife, for he had outwitted the gods again. Sisyphus lived a long and happy life. Finally, he died of old age and made his final journey to the Underworld, escorted by Hermes. This time Hades was prepared for him and took him to a steep hill.

Hades: Sisyphus, I have waited many years for you to die. Now I am going to give you a task to do. See the boulder at the bottom of the hill? Your job is to push it to the top. Get to work and don't quit until you are finished.

Narrator 2: Sisyphus pushed the boulder up the hill, but when he got close to the top, the boulder slipped from his hands and rolled to the bottom again. Sisyphus spent eternity trying to complete the task Hades had set for him. He never had time to think of new tricks again.

ZEUS AND HERA

Hera's name means "protectress" in Greek. Zeus cajoled Hera into marrying him, even though Hera knew that Zeus could not remain true to one wife. She watched him constantly and discovered him hiding in a cloud with Io. To avoid being found out, Zeus changed Io into a pure white heifer. Hera had her servant Argus, who had one hundred eyes, watch over Io. But Zeus sent his son Hermes to free Io. Hermes tricked Argus into falling asleep, releasing Io, who fled to Egypt. Io gave birth to Zeus's son, whom Hera kidnapped. But Io found him, and they returned to Egypt, where she married the king.

Presentation Suggestions

The narrators can be sitting on either side of the stage. Zeus should be in the center with Hera on his immediate right and Io on his immediate left. Hermes and Argus can stand slightly to the back of Hera and Io.

Props

The stage could be decorated with peacock feathers. A mural showing the relationship of Greece to Egypt could decorate that back of the stage. The characters could dress in appropriate clothing, with Argus perhaps wearing a shirt covered with eyes.

Delivery Suggestions

Hera should sound jealous and angry with Zeus when confronting him about his escapades. Zeus should sound persuasive and charming. Argus should sound obedient with Hera and pleased for Hermes's company. Hermes should sound congenial.

Characters

- ▣ Narrator 1
- ▣ Hera
- ▣ Narrator 2
- ▣ Zeus
- ▣ Argus
- ▣ Hermes

ZEUS AND HERA

Narrator 1: When Zeus fell in love with Hera and proposed marriage, she at first refused him. She resented his practice of taking mortal wives and wanted no part of his rule. But Zeus wanted Hera for himself and was not to be dissuaded. He created a thunderstorm and changed himself into a little cuckoo bird, flying into her arms for protection.

Hera: Your poor little bird, let me warm you.

Narrator 2: Zeus changed back to his godly form, and Hera found herself hugging him.

Hera: Zeus! You tricked me!

Zeus: Hera, you know I'm not going to give up until you marry me, so you might as well agree now.

Hera: I'll marry you, Zeus, but I'm warning you not to make me angry. No more wives, Zeus!

Zeus: You know I'll be true to you, Hera. Now let's prepare for the wedding!

Narrator 1: The wedding was glorious, with all the flowers and trees in bloom to celebrate. But no matter how hard he tried, Zeus couldn't remain true to Hera. He would sneak down to Greece and marry mortal girls while assuming various disguises. He believed that his heirs would inherit his greatness, which could only benefit Greece. Hera was greatly displeased with his philandering practices.

Hera: Zeus, you haven't changed at all. You think that I don't know what you are doing, but I'm always watching you.

Zeus: Hera, you know that the sun rises and sets with you!

Narrator 2: But Hera wasn't convinced of his fidelity and continued to watch Zeus. One day she spied a dark cloud on Earth and became suspicious. She rushed to the cloud, and just as she suspected, she found Zeus. To her surprise, he was holding a little pure white heifer.

Hera: Zeus, what a lovely little heifer. Won't you let me have it?

Narrator 1: Hera suspected that the heifer was Zeus's latest conquest, and indeed it was Io, a lovely young girl. Zeus was caught in his ruse, but he had to pretend that the heifer meant nothing to him.

Zeus: Of course, Hera, you are welcome to the cow.

Narrator 2: Hera tied the heifer to a tree and called for her servant, the giant Argus.

Hera: Argus, I have a task for you. I have tied a little white heifer to the tree in the garden. Use your hundred eyes to make sure that she doesn't get away.

Argus: As you wish, Hera.

Narrator 1: With his hundred eyes, Argus made an excellent watchman, never closing more than half of his eyes at any given time. But he was accustomed to more excitement in his life and watching a cow quickly bored him. Meanwhile, Zeus was plotting to free Io by enlisting the help of his son, Hermes.

Zeus: Hermes, find a way to set Io free. Argus is guarding her, but I know you can figure out how to get by him.

Hermes: Father, I'll be glad to try. Just watch what I do.

Narrator 2: Hermes disguised himself as a flute-playing shepherd, and he went to see Argus.

Hermes: Good morning, Argus. You look like you could use some company.

Argus: You're right about that, young man. A bit of conversation and music would be welcome.

Hermes: Let me play for you, and then perhaps a story would pass the time.

Argus: That would surely help keep me entertained, my friend.

Narrator 1: After playing his flute for a while, Hermes began to tell a tedious story. Soon fifty of Argus's eyes had closed in sleep. As Hermes persisted with his endless story, the other fifty eyes began to droop. When all one hundred eyes were closed, Hermes cut off Argus's head, leaving his eyes closed for all of eternity.

Hermes: Io, I am going to untie you, but I can't break the spell on you. Run home to your father.

Narrator 2: Io ran home, but her father didn't recognize her. She could only moo, so she finally scratched the letters *I* and *O* in the sand with her hoof, and her father realized what had happened. He flew at Zeus in a rage, but Zeus threw down a thunderbolt to ward him off. Meanwhile, Hera realized that Argus was dead and Io was free.

Hera: Io, I'm not done with you yet. I'm sending a gadfly to pester you to death. As for Argus, he may be dead, but I'm going to ensure that he isn't forgotten. His eyes will be put on the peacock's tail, and everyone will admire its beauty forevermore.

Narrator 1: The eyes of Argus were still unseeing, but they looked gorgeous on the peacock, which became quite vain as a result. Meanwhile, Io ran all over Greece, trying to escape from the stinging gadfly.

Narrator 2: Finally, Io ran to Egypt, where the people marveled at her pure white form and worshiped her.

Zeus: Hera, can't you leave Io alone? Look at how you've tormented her, chasing her all the way to Egypt.

Hera: All right, Zeus, I suppose you can change her back to human form now, but you are to have nothing else to do with her. Promise me you'll never look at her again.

Zeus: I promise, and I'll see that she stays in Egypt.

Narrator: Io did stay in Egypt, giving birth to Zeus's son Epaphus. When Hera heard about the birth, she had the child kidnapped. But Io searched for her son, who was being raised by the wife of the king of Byblos, in Syria. She found him and returned to Egypt, where she eventually married the king, Telegonus. She lived in Egypt happily, enjoying the respect of the people.

 **BIBLIOGRAPHY**

Books

Aeschylus. *Prometheus Bound.* New York: Dover, 1995.

Bierlein, J. F. *Parallel Myths.* New York: Ballantine Publishing Group, 1994.

Blaisdell, Bob. *Favorite Greek Myths.* Illustrated by John Green. New York: Dover, 1996.

Bulfinch, Thomas. *Bulfinch's Mythology.* New York: Harper & Row, 1970.

Cottrell, Arthur. *A Dictionary of World Mythology.* New York: G. P. Putnam's Sons, 1979.

D'Aulaire, Ingri, and Edgar Parin D'Aulaire. *Book of Greek Myths.* Garden City, NY: Doubleday, 1999.

Geringer, Laura. *Atalanta: The Wild Girl.* Illustrated by Peter Bollinger. New York: Scholastic, 1997.

Graves, Robert. *The Greek Myths: 1.* New York: Penguin, 1993.

———. *The Greek Myths: 2.* New York: Penguin, 1993.

Grimal, Pierre. *The Dictionary of Classical Mythology.* Malden, Mass.: Blackwell Publishers, 1996.

Hamilton, Edith. *Mythology: Timeless Tales of Gods and Heroes.* Boston: Little, Brown and Company, 1999.

Lattimore, Deborah Nourse. *Medusa.* New York: HarperCollins, 2000.

Lies, Betty. *Earth's Daughters: Stories of Women in Classical Mythology.* Golden, Colo.: Fulcrum Publishing, 1999.

McLaren, Clemence. *Waiting for Odysseus.* New York: Simon & Schuster, 2000.

Mitchell, Adrian. *The Odyssey.* Illustrated by Stuart Robinson. New York: DK Publishing, 2000.

New Larousse Encyclopedia of Mythology. Translated by Richard Aldington and Delano Ames. New York: Hamlyn Publishing Group, 1973.

O'Connolly, Peter. *The Ancient Greece of Odysseus.* New York: Oxford University Press, 1999.

Orgel, Doris. *The Princess and the God.* New York: Orchard Books, 1996.

———. *We Goddesses: Athena, Aphrodite, Hera.* Illustrated by Marilee Heyer. New York: DK Publishing, 1999.

Philip, Neil. *The Adventures of Odysseus.* Illustrated by Peter Malone. New York: Orchard Books, 1997.

Schwab, Gustav. *Gods and Heroes: Myths and Epics of Ancient Greece.* New York: Pantheon Books, 1974.

Spires, Elizabeth. *I Am Arachne.* Illustrated by Mordicai Gerstein. New York: Farrar, Straus & Giroux, 2001.

Stephanides, Menelaos. *The Gods of Olympus.* Toronto: Sigma, 1999.

Switzer, Ellen, and Costas. *Greek Myths: Gods, Heroes, and Monsters: Their Sources, Their Stories, and Their Meanings.* New York: Atheneum, 1988.

Tripp, Edward. *The Meridian Handbook of Classical Mythology.* New York: Penguin, 1974.

Walker, Barbara G. *The Women's Encyclopedia of Myths and Secrets.* New York: Harper & Row, 1983.

Weigle, Marta. *Spiders and Spinsters: Women and Mythology.* Albuquerque, N. Mex.: University of New Mexico Press, 1982.

Yolen, Jane, and Robert J. Harris. *Odysseus and the Serpent Maze.* New York: HarperCollins, 2001.

Video

Moyers, Bill. *Joseph Campbell and the Power of Myth.* New York: Mystic Five Video, 1988. Six videocassettes, 360 minutes.

Web Sites

http://genealogy.ijp.si/gedcom/antika/
Includes a listing of more than 1,500 surnames.

http://www.greekmythology.com/
Includes family tree, gods, Titans, myths, figures, creatures, places, heroes, and books.

http://library.thinkquest.org/18650/
Multimedia presentation of art, constellations, gods, stories, monsters, and others.

http://www.messagenet.com/myths/
Includes brief introductions, comparisons of Greek and Roman names, various links.

Abderus (ăb'•də•rəs)

Achelous (ăk•ə•lō'əs)

Acheron (ăk'ə•rŏn)

Achilles (ə•kĭl'ēz)

Acrisius (ə•krĭs'ĭəs)

Acropolis (ə•krŏp'ə•lĭs)

Actaeon (ăk•tē'ŏn)

Acustus (ă•kəs'təs)

Admete (ăd•mē'tē)

Admetus (ăd•mē'təs)

Adrastus (ə•drăs'təs)

Aeëtes (ē•ē'tēz)

Agamemnon (ăg'•ə•měm'nŏn)

Aegean (ĭ•jē'ən)

Aegeus (ē'jūs)

Aegina (ē•jĭ'nə)

Aegyptus (ē•jĭp'təs)

Aeneas (ē•nē'əs)

Aeolus (ē'ə•ləs)

Aeson (ē'sən)

Alcmene (ălk•mē'nē)

Amazon (ăm'ə•zŏn)

Amphion (ăm•fī'ŏn)

Amphitryon (ăm•fīt'rĭ•ŏn)

Amphythaon (ăm•fī•thā'ən)

Anatha (ə•nă'thə)

Anchises (ăn•kī'sēz)

Andromeda (ăn•drŏm'ə•də)

Antaeus (ăn•tē•əs)

Antigone (ăn•tĭg'ə•nē)

Aphrodite (ăf•rō•dī'tē)

Apollo (ə•pŏl'ō)

Arachne (ə•răk'nē)

Arcadia (ar•kā'dĭ•ə)

Areopagus (ăr'ē•ŏp'ə•gəs)

Ares (ā'rēz)

Argo (ar'gō)

Argonauts (ar'gə•nautz)

Argos (ar'gŏs)

Argus (ar'gəs)

Ariadne (ĕr•ĭ•ăd'nē)

Aristaeus (ĕr•ĭs•tē'əs)

Artemis (ar'tə•mĭs)

Ascalaphus (ăs•kăl'ə•fəs)

Ascanius (ăs•kā'nĭ•əs)

Asclepius (ăs•klē'pĭ•əs)

Asopus (ə•sō'pəs)

Astraeus (ăs•trē'əs)

Atalanta (ăt•ə•lăn'tə)

Athamus (ăth'ə•məs)

Athena (ə•thē'nə)

Athene (ə•thē'nē)

Athenian (ă•thē'nē•ən)

Athens (ăth'nz)

Atlas (ăt'ləs)

Attica (ăt'ĭ•kə)

Augias (au•jē'əs)

Autolycus (au•tŏl'ĭ•kəs)

Bacchus (băk'əs)

Balius (bā'lĭ•əs)

Bias (bī•əs)

Bithynia (bĭ•thĭn'ĭ•ə)

Boeötia (bē•ō'shĭ•ə)

Boreas (bō'rē•əs)

Byblos (bīb'ləs)

Calabria (kə•lā'brē•ə)

Calliope (kə•lī'ə•pē)

Calydonia (kăl•ə•dōn'ē•ə)

Cassandra (kŭ•săn'drə)

Cassiopeia (kăs•ĭ•ō•pē'ə)

Castor (kăs'ter)

Caucasus (kô'kă•səs)

Cecrops (sē'krŏps)

Celeüs (sē'lĭ•əs)

Centaur (sĕn'taur)

Cepheus (sē'fūs)

Cerberus (ser'bə•rəs)

Ceres (sēr'ēz)

Chalybes (kăl'ĭ•bēz)

Charybdis (kə•rĭb'dĭs)

Chione (kī'ō•nē)

Chiron (kī'rən)

Chrysaor (krĭ•sā'ŏr)

Circe (ser'sē)

Clio (klē'ō)

Clymene (klĭm'ə•nē)

Clytemnestra (klī•təm•něs'trə)

Coeüs (sē'əs)

Colcalus (kŏl'kə•ləs)

Colchis (kŏl'kĭs)

Colonus (kə•lō'nəs)

Corinth (kŏr'ĭnth)

Creon (krē'ŏn)

Crete (krē'tē)

Cretheus (krē'thūs)

Creüsa (krē•ū'sə)

Cronus (krō'nəs)

Cyclopes (sī•klō'pēz)

Cyllene (sĭ•lĕ'nē)

Cyzicus (sĭz'ĭ•kəs)

Daedalus (dĕd'l•əs)

Danaë (dăn'ā•ē)

Danaïdes (də•nā'ĭ•dēz')

Danaüs (dăn'ā•əs)

Deïaneira (dē•ə•nī'rə)

Delos (dē'lŏs)

Delphi (dĕl'fī)

Demeter (dē•mē'ter)

Demophon (dē•mə•fun)

Deucalion (dū•kā'lĭ•ən)

Dictys (dĭk'tĭs)

Diomedes (dī•ō•mē'dēz)

Dione (dī•ō'nē)

Dionysus (dī•ō•nī'səs)

Dodona (dō•dō'nə)

Doliones (dō•lē•ō'nēz)

Dryad (drī'ăd)

Echidna (ē•kĭd'nə)

Echo (ĕk'ō)

Eleusis (ē•lū'sĭs)

Emathion (ē•mā'thī•ŏn)

Endymion (ĕn•dĭm'ĭ•ŏn)

Eos (ē'ŏs)

Epimetheus (ĕp•ĭ•mē'thūs)

Erato (ĕr'ə•tō)

Erginus (ĕr•jī'nəs)

Erinyes (ē•rĭn'ĭ•ēz)

Eros (ē'rŏs)

Erymanthus (ĕr•ĭ•măn'thəs)

Erythia (ĕ•rĭ•thī'ə)

Eteocles (ē•tē'ō•klēz)

Ethiopia (ē•thĭ•ō'pĭ•ə)

Eumolpus (u•mŏl'pəs)

Euphemus (ū'fə•məs)

Eurus (ūr'ŭs)

Eurydice (ū•rĭd'ĭ•sē)

Eurystheus (ū•rĭs'thē•əs)

Eurytion (ū•rĭt'ĭ•ŏn)

Euterpe (ū•ter'pē)

Euxine (uk'sĭn)

Gaderia (gă•dēr'ē•ə)

Gaia (gā'ə)

Gaul (gŏl)

Geryon (jē•rī'ŏn)

Glauce (glau'sē)

Gorgon (gŏr'gən)

Hades (hā'dēz)

Hecate (hĕk'ə•tĕ)

Hecuba (hĕk'ū•bə)

Hegieia (hĕ•jē'ē•ə)

Helen (hĕl•ən)

Helios (hē'lē•əs)

Heliades (hē•lī'ə•dēz)

Helle (hĕl'ē)

Hephaestus (hē•fĕs'təs)

Hera (hē'rə)

Heracles (hĕr'ə•klēz)

Hercules (her'kū•lēz)

Hermes (her'mēz)

Hermione (hur•mī'ə•nē)

Hesione (hĕ •sī'ō•nē)

Hippolyta (hĭ•pŏl'ĭ•tə)

Hippolytus (hĭ•pŏl'ĭ•təs)

Hyacinthus (hī•ə•sĭn'thəs)

Hyades (hī'ə•dēz)

Hydra (hī'drə)

Hygeia (hī•jē'ə)

Hylas (hī'ləs)

Hyperion (hī'pĭr'ĭ•ən)

Hypermnestra (hī•perm•nĕs'trə)

Hypsipyle (hĭp•sĭp'ĭ•lē)

Iasus (ī'ə•səs)

Iberia (ī•bĭr'ē•ə)

Icarus (ĭk'ə•rəs)

Idomene (ī•dŏ•mē'nē)

Ilithyia (ĭ•lĭ'thē•ə)

Ino (ī'nō)

Io (ī'ō)

Iolaus (ī•ō•lā'ə•s)

Iolcus (ī•ŏl'kəs)

Iphicles (ĭf'ĭ•klēz)

Iris (ī'rĭs)

Ismene (ĭs•mē'nē)

Ister (ĭs'ter)

Ixion (ĭk•zī'ŏn)

Jocasta (jō•kăs'tə)

Kore (kō'rē)

Labyrinthe (lăb'ə•rĭnth)

Laïus (lā'ĭ•əs)

Laomedon (lā•ŏm'ə•dŏn)

Lapith (lăp'ĭth)

Leda (lē'də)

Lemnos (lĕm'nŏs)

Lesbos (lĕz'bŏs)

Leto (lē'tō)

Libya (lĭb'ĭ•ə)

Liguria (lĭ•gū'rĭ•ə)

Linus (lī'nəs)

Lydia (lĭd'ĭ•ə)

Lynceus (lĭn'sus)

Maia (mī'ə)

Marsyas (mar'sī•əs)

Medea (mē•dē'ə)

Medusa (mĭ•dou'sə)

Megara (mĕg'ə•rə)

Melampus (mə•lăm'pəs)

Melanion (mə•lā'nĭ•ŏn)

Melanippe (mĕl•ə•nĭp'ē)

Meleager (mĕl•ē•ā'jer)

Melpomene (mĕl•pŏm'ĭ•nē)

Memnon (mĕm'nŏn)

Menelaus (mĕn•ə•lā'əs)

Menoetius (mə•nē'shĭ•əs)

Merope (mĕr'ō•pē)

Messenia (mə•sē'nĭ•ə)

Metaneira (mĕt'ə•nē'rə)

Metis (mē'tĭs)

Midas (mī'dəs)

Minos (mī'nŏs)

Minotaur (mĭn'ə•taur)

Mnemosyne (nē•mŏz'ĭ•nē)

Mycenae (mī•sē'nē)

Mysia (mĭsh'ĭ•ə)

Narcissus (nar•sĭs'əs)

Naxos (năk'sŏs)

Neleus (nē'lūs)

Nephele (nĕf'ə•lē)

Nereids (nē'rĭ•ĭds)

Nereus (nēr'us)

Nessus (nĕs'əs)

Nike (nī'kē)

Niobe (nī'ə•bē)

Notus (nō'təs)

Nysa (nī'sə)

Odysseus (ō•dĭs'ūs)

Oedipus (ĕd'ĭ•pəs)

Oeneus (ē'nūs)

Oenopion (ē•nō'pĭ•ŏn)

Olympus (ō•lĭm'pəs)

Omphale (ŏm'fə•lē)

Onchestus (ŏn•kĕs'təs)

Orchomenus (or•kŏm'ə•nəs)

Orion (ō•rī'ən)

Orpheus (ŏr'fus, or'fĭ•əs)

Ortygia (ŏr•tĭj'ĭ'ĭ•ə)

Pactolus (păk•tō'ləs)

Pallas (păl'əs)

Pan (păn)

Pandora (păn•dō'rə)

Paris (pĕr'ĭs)

Parnassus (par•nu'əs)

Parthenius (par•thē'nĭ•əs)

Pasiphaë (pə•sĭf'ā•ē)

Pegasus (pĕg'ə•səs)

Pelias (pē'lĭ•əs)

Pelops (pē'lŏps)

Penelope (pə•nĕl'ə•pē)

Peparethus (pĕ•pă•rē'thəs)

Pero (pē'rō)

Persephone (per•sĕf'ə•nē)

Perseus (per'sus)

Phaëthon (fa'ə•thŏn)

Phasis (fā'sĭs)

Philoctetes (fĭl•ŏk•tē'tēz)

Phineus (fĭ'nūs)

Phoebe (fē'bē)

Phrixus (frĭk'səs)

Phrygia (frĭj'ĭ•ə)

Phylacus (fī'lə•kəs)

Pirithous (pī•rĭth'ō•əs)

Pitys (pīt'ĭs)

Pleiades (plē'ə•dēz)

Pleione (plī•ō'nē)

Pluto (ploo'tō)

Pollux (pŏl'əks)

Polybus (pŏl'ĭ•bəs)

Polydectes (pŏl•ĭ•dĕk'tēz)

Polyhymnia (pŏl•ĭ•hĭm'nĭ•ə)

Polynices (pŏl•ĭ•nī'sēz)

Poseidon (pə•sī'dŏn)

Priam (prī'əm)

Prometheus (prō•mē'thūs, prō•mē'thĭ•əs)

Proserpina (prō•ser'pĭ•nə)

Proteus (prō'tūs, prō'tĭ•əs)

Psyche (sī'kē)

Pyrrha (pĭr'ə)

Pythian (pĭth'ĭ•ən)

Rhadamanthys (răd•ə•măn'thĭs)

Scylla (sĭl'ə)

Scythian (sĭth'ĭ•ən)

Selene (sē•lē'nē)

Semele (sĕm'ə•lē)

Seriphus (sə•rī'fəs)

Sicily (sĭs'ĭ•lē)

Silenus (sī•lē'nəs)

Sirens (sī'rənz)

Sisyphus (sĭs'ĭ•fəs)

Sparta (spar'tə)

Sphinx (sfĭnks)

Staphylus (stăf'ĭ•ləs)

Stymphalus (stĭm•fā'ləs)

Styx (stĭks)

Symplegades (sĭm•plĕg'ə•dēz)

Syrinx (sĭr'ĭngks)

Talos (tā'ləs)

Tantalus (tăn'tə•ləs)

Telegonus (tē•lĕg'ə•nəs)

Terpsichore (terp•sĭk'ə•rē)

Teutarus (tū•tar'əs)

Thalia (thə•lī'ə)

Thanatos (thăn'ə•tŏs)

Thebes (thēbz)

Thebus (thē'bəs)

Theia (thē'ə)

Themiscyra (thĕm•ĭs•kī'rə)

Theseus (thē'sūs, thē'sĭ•əs)

Thespius (thĕs'pĭ•əs)

Thessaly (thĕs'ə•lē)

Thetis (thē'tĭs)

Thoas (thō'ăs)

Thrace (thrās)

Tiresias (tī•rē'sĭ•əs)

Titan (tī'tən)

Tithonus (tĭ•thō'nəs)

Triptolemus (trĭp•tŏl'ə•məs)

Tyndareus (tĭn•dĕr'ĭ•əs)

Typhon (tī'fōn)

Urania (ū•rā•nĭ•ə)

Uranus (ū'rə•nəs)

Xerxes (zerk'zē z)

Zephyrus (zĕf'ə•rəs)

Zeus (zūs, zoos)

 # INDEX OF NAMES AND PLACES

Suzanne I. Barchers is the author of twenty teacher resource and textbooks and more than twenty books for children. She earned a doctorate of education in curriculum and instruction at the University of Colorado, Boulder. After working as a teacher and administrator in public and private schools for fifteen years, she began a second career in publishing and as an affiliate faculty member at the University of Colorado, Denver. Since 1999, Barchers has been Managing Editor at Weekly Reader in Stamford, Connecticut, commuting between Stamford and her home in Arvada, Colorado. You can find other books by Barchers at www.storycart.com.

from *Teacher Ideas Press*

CELEBRATING THE EARTH: Stories, Experiences, Activities
Norma J. Livo

Invite young readers to observe, explore, and appreciate the natural world through engaging activities. Livo shows you how to use folk stories, personal narrative, and a variety of learning projects to teach students about amphibians, reptiles, mammals, constellations, plants, and other natural phenomena. Designed to build a Naturalist Intelligence in young learners, these stories and activities are packed with scientific information. **All Levels.**
xvii, 174p. 8½x11 paper ISBN 1-56308-776-6

FAMOUS PROBLEMS AND THEIR MATHMATICIAN
Art Johnson

Why did ordering an omelet cost one mathematician his life? The answer to this and other questions are found in this exciting new resource that shows your students how 60 mathematicians discovered mathematical solutions through everyday situations. These lessons are easily incorporated into the curriculum as an introduction to a math concept, a homework piece, or an extra challenge. Teacher notes and suggestions for the classroom are followed by extension problems and additional background material. **Grades 5–12.**
xvi, 179p. 8½x11 paper ISBN 1-56308-446-5

SCIENCE AND MATH BOOKMARK BOOK: 300 Fascinating, Fact-Filled Bookmarks
Kendall Haven and Roni Berg

Use these 300 reproducible bookmarks of fascinating facts, concepts, trivia, inventions, and discoveries to spark student learning. They cover all major disciplines of math and physical, earth, and life sciences—ready to copy, cut out, and give to your students. **Grades 4 and up.**
xii, 115p. 8½x11 paper ISBN 1-56308-675-1

WRITE RIGHT! Creative Writing Using Storytelling Techniques
Kendall Haven

Haven's breakthrough approach to creative writing uses storytelling techniques to enhance the creative writing process. This practical guide offers you directions for 38 writing exercises that will show students how to create powerful and dynamic fiction. All the steps are included, from finding inspiration and creating believable characters to the final edit. Activities are coded by levels, but most can be adapted to various grades. **All Levels.**
240p. 8½x11 paper ISBN 1-56308-677-8

VISUAL MESSAGES: Integrating Imagery into Instruction
2d Edition
David M. Considine and Gail E. Haley

The authors provide effective media literacy strategies, activities, and resources that help students learn the critical-viewing skills necessary in our media-dominated world. Various media and types of programs are addressed, including motion pictures, television news, and advertising. Activities are coded by grade level and curriculum area. **Grades K–12.**
xxiii,371p. 8½x11 paper ISBN 1-56308-575-5

For a free catalog or to place an order, please contact:
Teacher Ideas Press
Dept. B051 • P.O. Box 6633 • Englewood, CO • 80155-6633
800-237-6124 • www.lu.com/tip • Fax: 303-220-8843